Walking into Spring, or
Bowling My Way Home...

An Appalachian Trail Story

Walking into Spring, or
Bowling My Way Home…

Enjoy! and it's been great visiting with your family love Dierdre 2012

Dierdre E. Dennis

She embraced town and wilderness experiences

to redefine her place in society.

This book is dedicated to *you*.

AKNOWLEDGEMENTS

I wish to thank the following friends and family for their love, support and thoughtful encouragement as I worked on this story.

Marianne; Ashtray, Cesar, Gourmet, Jester, Ms. Janet, Pan and You; Caitlin, Jacob and Lucas Dennis-DeVries; David and Nancy Dennis; David, Karen, Douglas, Joyce, Dwight and Donna Dennis; Chris, Donna and Heidi; Randy and Lisa; Ann, Peter and Michael.

Tonys in Gatlinburg, Victory Lanes, Franklin Lanes, all A.T Outfitters and Trail Angels everywhere! Curtis, Standing Bear Hostel, and the community of '02 hikers (you know who you are!) that collectively enriched my walk.

Punos and Mountain.

"When you come to the edge of all you know,
You must believe in one of two things,
There will be earth upon which to stand,
Or you will be given wings."

Unknown Author

> *"Once you are out the door, the hardest part of the journey is behind you."*
>
> *Unknown Author*

Walking to reclaim some sense of purpose will hopefully open the door to a self- discovery beyond any preconceived expectations.

And so it was, from the moment I stepped off of the front porch, of my cozy little post and beam home in Vermont, got into a white rental car laden with all the appropriate hiking gear and drove further away from the foothills than I'd ever been in any one year, that this story has its beginnings….

And no mind here to the particulars… for what led up to this is of no consequence, barring only that, at this juncture, I was a person becoming unglued and all conventional methods of rerouting emotional behavior had been lost, lost until one morning when you asked a pivotal question that would forever change my view of life. This word, the sum of several letters, to your question was: *yes.*

This *yes,* would be the seed of an unfolding journey that would have me leaving all known securities to make yet, another attempt to find the answer, or at least a clue as to what my direction truly might be.

"This journey," you said, "would be along one of the country's most famous and well worn wooded paths: The Appalachian Trail."

No turning back now.

I was soon to be walking, nothing more and nothing less, just walking….

But, before this walking could begin several details had to be addressed.

Being the type of person I am, I realized that I needed a plan of another sort. A more tangible focus, and one, other than myself. A painter and colorist by craft, I would lose my color.

Ah, Yes! That would do. I will take black and white photographs and describe the corresponding colors in my journal.

The wholeness of the ensuing walk *was,* with each passing day, becoming clearer. I *was* ready, to part, with all that I held dear.

...*and then*, we have a week of last meals, which include, several lobster and corn lunches, multi shopping trips to the outfitter, buying, weighing and packing bump boxes, renting a car and saying our goodbyes to a multitude of friends and family, some of whom, were still trying, while respecting my unsettledness, to understand: *why? Why* I would want to spend several months in the woods, let alone one night!

Anyway, with that done, it is here and now, that this story truly begins, as recorded in a simple, purple leather bound journal

....and what follows is a snapshot of a woman

on a path,
eerily familiar and yet,
unfamiliar,
to a destination
once met
she'd long for over
and over again

Monday April 1, 2002

Destination: Georgia. Distance: 1134.37 miles. Time: 19.8 hrs.

It's eleven P.M. and we are heading south.

"Is it 91 we're on?" I ask.

"Yes," you answer.

Soon this dialogue quickly reverses, to you asking and me answering your gazillion questions.

My initial alertness subsides. I become tired of thinking and hearing myself talk and wondering, not wanting to be disrespectful, when in God's name you'd run out of questions!

This was, whether you knew it or not, the beginning of a cleansing process. All your questions were taking all my words.

The first leg of this journey includes stopping in Springfield, Massachusetts to pick up a knit hat for you, bowling in Newington, Ct. at 2:11 A.M., New York City at dawn and then, onto the Jersey Turnpike.

Tuesday April 2, 2002. New York City

Ambivalent or better stated: Scared! I feel nauseous.

"I have to use the bathroom."

To which you reply, "I could use a Spanish omelet. I think there is a diner…"

"Stop the car!" I said, "Now!"

"Jesus, D!" you exclaim and immediately pull up alongside the curb.

I quickly get out of the car, no shoes on my feet and go directly into a Laundromat.

"Do you have a bathroom?" I ask.

"Yes," the attendant replies, and barely looking up from his newspaper, he hands me the key.

Chained to a wood block is the key to my relief! So I do my thing and in exiting the ladies room, I extend my key - holding hand to him. His eyes are still down, as he points toward the top of his Whirlpool washers and solemnly says, "Just put it there."

I look at him for a moment. Then, I gently set the wood-chained key down on one of his mustard-colored machines; thank him, and still shoeless, walk out the door. In the mean time, you had found your Spanish omelet-making diner.

> *downtown*
> whose feet ran down this street?
> whose body ached, with pain-unaided?
> whose flesh lies still
> beneath debris picked clean and sifted dry?
> whose eyes were wide, in disbelief,
> that final moment?

Ground Zero: The hole in the ground.

I just don't know what to say about the flag on the adjacent structure, the black netting draped across the buildings, the security, the viewing platform, the loss of thousands….

So, I guess, I just said it! This space, which I had only seen on CNN-TV, would now and forever more, be all too real to me.

Art Note Reflection: The face paintings I did last fall are a direct result of this action.

They are the only pieces to date, which are directly related to an historical event with emotional consequences. To me these pieces are frighteningly rich.

> *bronze garden*
> it was there
> that I read,
> from across a lambent pool of light
> "for a fallen soldier knows no color"

Traffic, police, security, truck upon truck of debris…. You drive around this site, too many times, in an effort to find the way to the Jersey Turnpike. Waiting in traffic, I sketch in my journal, until the light changes and we move onward. Once in New Jersey we stop at the Visitors Center to make a phone call or two.

Deep breath… It's hot. Public bathrooms are awful! I've only had a few hours of sleep. Mental whining…

"Do you want to drive?" you ask.

"Sure," I reluctantly respond.

Behind the wheel now, I pull out of the lot.

"Would this be the Jersey Turnpike we're on?" I blurt out; boding a questionable confidence that warrants no comment from you.

I am beyond the point where I can turn back.

Driving is such a strange experience when you've had so little sleep and, I'm guessing now, several cups of bad coffee, in between the good.

I talk, even though you're asleep and proceed to tell you, among other things, that I once drove a twenty four foot U-Haul across the Chesapeake Bay Bridge and that I got this, " I'm going to jump" feeling when I looked down at the water.

Guess you really weren't sleeping, 'cause you surprise me and say, "D. Do you feel it *now*?"

I say, "I don't know. I haven't looked at the water, yet."

To that, you sternly reply, "Then, ***Don't.*** OK?"

Our next stop: The Wildlife Refuge and The Decoy Museum.

This is a great place to take a much needed break. We walk around the refuge, eat a sandwich, and take pictures of each other out on the pier.

The Decoy Museum is totally random, but what one checks out, when they're at a Wildlife Refuge and their name is D!

The Blue Ridge Parkway, the Winery, the Olive Garden Restaurant……and, did I mention bowling?

Plus, a random comment *"It's not quite gospel, but its right next door"* from a predawn radio talk-show Korean Methodist.

What exactly does that imply when you are sleeping in a gas station parking lot?

Driving Miss D…Food… Sleeping…. Bowling….

<u>Wednesday April 3, 2002 Elliston, Va. Gas station. 7:34 A.M.</u>

Yes, bowling! Victory Lanes in Newington that first night and now, Triangle Lanes, Christiansburg, Va., which happens to be right off route 81.

This is something so random and yet, fun to do.

We both bowl a minimum of three games. In Virginia, the guy let us pick out our own music and I have a ball that I should buy! When we are getting ready to leave, the manager comes out to the parking lot to see how heavy our packs are.

Drive a bit before stopping at a gas station near the Shenandoah Parkway. It is 2:20 A.M. We sleep in the car.

In the morning I sketch a picture of the house next to the parking lot.

Gas stations have bathrooms, coffee, and cranberry juice! All the amenities for parking lot campers!

From the gas station, we drive a couple of miles to a local winery. No visible signs of personnel, so we give ourselves the tour. With coffees in hand, we proudly walk the vineyard, as if it is our own.

Continuing on… The Blue Ridge Parkway… very windy… You stop the car at almost every pull off to take in the view.

As we come off the parkway we stop by a stream, cook a little, and because you are tired, you unload all our gear, take out the back seat, hop in the newly enlarged open trunk, and sleep. I wash in the stream and wait. You are a very good sleeper.

A car stops. A couple seeking directions… I barely know where we are, but try to be helpful.

They inquire about the person in the trunk to which I reply, "He's okay, just sleeping."

I continue to write until you awake, where upon I relay the story.

We pack up and drive on.

An Asian Restaurant in the afternoon somewhere, then it's on to returning the car in Atlanta, Ga., mailing our bump boxes, and hooking up with a local guy who transports hikers to the trailhead.

Thursday April 4, 2002. Atlanta, Georgia. Postcard Home:

Hi everybody. I'm missing you a lot! I am in Atlanta, Georgia. Just mailed the drop boxes and got this card at Borders. I'm about to return the car and get a bus to Amicalola Falls State Park and begin the journey. You might not hear from me for a week. So, lot's of hugs and kisses for everyone. Thanks, again, for all the faith and support in me and helping me move ahead with this trip. This is so perfect! Take Care.

We drive to the airport, turn in our car and the pay big bucks for what, I had originally thought would be a money saver, is now *smokin'* my credit card! Oh well…..life without a car….

Did I mention that my pack weighs in at 45 pounds, *and*, that I've actually never walked with it on *and* I can't even put it on by myself, let alone take it off once it's on….

So, with this in mind, we walk from the Atlanta airport towards the train station in the 80 degree southern heat.

A 45 pound pack and non collapsible poles are highly unmanageable in these crowded cars, but I'm trying.

Riding the train to the end of the line, where upon we hook up with our driver. In the station parking lot, tired and unshowered, I drop my pack. No finesse here.

The top of my Nalgene bottle cracks and I think: *sure I'm going to hike. I can't even deal with this pack in an urban setting! Keep laughing!*

We meet a woman who just happens to be from Woodstock, VT.!

Small world!

Finally, the white Toyota arrives. We get in. Our driver, *a local*, is a wild pig hunter who shuttles hikers for extra money.

The white Toyota, complete with a well- stocked gun rack, is from Africa.

I am tired.

A quick stop at a convenience store, then we are on our way to the trailhead.

Amicolola Falls State Park: 1700'

A place where we can camp…

Now, where we are is *not* the true trailhead. It is a place that our driver tells us is on private property, right off the A.T. access trail.

"You *should* be okay," he says.

It is dusk now and we begin to set up camp. Whose good timing is this anyway? Very soon it will be dark …. And, there are things to do, like….

…start a fire, cook some food, take a pee, find my headlamp and not feel *weird about wearing it!*

So, here we are settling in under the stars, when the property caretaker drives by. From the comfort of his truck, he calls to us, "You are camping on private property and should move or, risk the law enforcement removing you."

"Okay, but what is the likely - hood of that happening?" you ask him.

"Hey, it's your choice," he says, before driving away.

Too tired to really care, we decide to stay put and take our chances.

My first night in the woods in Georgia…

It's cold and dark and I'm what seems like, a million miles from home…..

Friday April 5, 2002. 6:28 A.M.

Upon awakening in the woods, my sense of place is once more redefined. I cannot see how I appear. I can only feel how I am.

This space seemed huge against the night sky, yet, by comparison, is quite small in the light of day.

Pumping Water: Off to the stream to figure out the filtration system. I am afraid. What if I do it wrong? What if it doesn't work? What if I take too long?

The resistance is not in pumping water, but to change and I think: *how will this simple act of pumping water change me?*

The campfire is a few feet away; the stream frigid and clear. …
…and here I am stooping down, pumping water, a task I find quite contemplative. It's working! Success!

Hey, I pumped the water! And then, I drink some right from the tube!

With all this flowing water, my next question is: Where am I to pee? Figure it out. Privacy, what's that? Find a big tree and take care of business.

If ever I was a lost child it is now. I know nothing. I want to look through my stuff over and over again, while I think: *"all [our] normal tendencies are lost in the process of domestication."*[1]

I just don't know what to do. I have so much to carry! So much will have to go at the first stop, such as the shirts, the mug, the juicer, the toiletry stuff. What I'll keep is the toothpaste, the Bronners, a blister kit and meds. ALL ELSE GOES!

…and now, you, with the experience of having already hiked a good portion of the trail several years ago, hold up my pack and I back myself into it.

You adjust the straps for me and ask, "How does it feel?"

"Good, I guess," I say, "for standing still."

"Pull the waist strap like *this* so the pack will set right." you tell me, as you do it.

"Okay." I reply.

With pack secure upon my back, I turn, take one last look at the ground, which held me last night and begin, …begin, walking … from the posted private property.

It is about five miles to a shelter and about another mile to the top of Springer Mountain.

I see yellow and purple violets, blood root, and trout lily. My pack feels pretty good, feet pretty sore, shoulders pretty achy….

Slowly, we are wending our way up a mountain: Springer Mt., to be exact …the southern terminus of the Appalachian Trail.

My shoulders ache. Did I already say this?

We reach this first peak, and with mixed emotions, I just stand and look out at the amazing view.

No words spoken.

You help me off with my 45 pound pack. Ah! This pack is going to *kill* me!

Springer Mountain: 3782'

The first peak…

I feel too scared to move from this 3782 foot sunlit spot.

This is where it all begins.

Day hikers and thru hikers mingle, share stories and start their trek in hopes of peaking Mount Katahdin in Maine come September.

No grand illusions here. My goal is: Hot Springs, North Carolina.

A minister from Ohio asks: "What brought you out here? Why would you leave home?" and then he adds, "I'll pray for your safety."

Pray for my safety. Well, I'd never thought that what I was about to do would warrant any ones prayers, but…

"Thank you," I say. "I'll send you my story."

There is something to be said about embarking on a journey into the wilderness with, hopefully, everything you need to survive, on your back and to have a minister say, he will pray for you. His is a gift which bears no weight.

Once again, you hold up my pack, as I back into it. Then, you adjust the straps. I fold and carefully place my neck warmer beneath the shoulder strap.

I touch the mountain stone, which bears the name Springer, and walk on…

Stover Creek Shelter: 2.5 miles from Springer Mountain

I drop my pack and lie on the picnic table and rest. You take a picture. Then, you help me back on with my pack and adjust the varied straps. I roll and fold the fleece hat and neck warmer, placing them with a gentle calculated ease under each shoulder before continuing…. for I've already bruised my arm just taking this pack off.

In a moment, the sun will be on my face.

As we begin to walk, I think: *You are the Earth. So connected... Like the hat on your head, reflecting the seasons of the land around us. These shades are the hues of my palette. They are the colors I long to feel upon my fingertips.*

Hawke Mountain Shelter: 7.6 miles from Springer Mountain.

Rigatoni and Angel Hair: a couple from Texas.

My thoughts are of eating…..
                              the wind caresses the hillside
                              much like a guest approaching the door

We prepare a dinner of noodles, rice, and beans. I add a little bit of my secret spice mix. *Red pepper flakes, garlic powder, basil, oregano, crazy Jane's pepper, salt, and dill.* Well, perhaps, a little *too* much! For when we take our first bites, pretty much at the same time, it is *way* too hot…gagging…. my throat is instantly on fire!

This is to be coupled with the fact that it is, well...*way* after our shelter mates have gone to bed… so, we not only have to be quiet, but we have to eat! Laughing, we force the food down between gulps of water. A great second night…

Did I mention the piece of sawdust that I got in my eye and the mice scurrying through my pack at night?

I think the night air is chilling my bones. I awake at 12:45, 2:30, and 4:40, and now it is 6:28. I feel quite shivery. Should I drink more water? Is that why I'm cold? Or is it something else? I am missing the weight of my home bed covers. My legs are shaking as I walk outside in the cool night air to pee. Upon returning to the warmth of my bag, my mind begins to chaotically roam on how much stupid stuff I brought and how I want to get rid of it all! Thirty pounds would be great! 45 lbs. IS WAY TOO HEAVY! Wish I had brought the hot chillys and thank God I brought the SUGOi's.

My top half is warm, my bottom half is not. And, as much as the shelter is providing protection from the wind, it is excessively hard on my hips.

I am missing the give of the ground….

The immediate plan: *I'll drink more water and try to sleep again. Now, my feet are warm, but legs are not. Figure that?*

> perhaps it is the wind calling my name
>
> in sleeplessness I hear the sound not present in a dream

Horse Gap: 2673' 10 miles from Springer Mountain

Hike a bit. Walk another 1.5 miles and decide to stop for the night.

Sleeping under the tarp of blue… howling winds… we are fogged in, and… out of water…..

Wake up at 6:15. Get the food down, coil the rope and pack my stuff.

No yard sale today 'cause I need water! What's a yard sale? Well, it's where I take everything out of my pack, spread it out on the ground, look at it, then systematically organize it and repack for the day.

It'll rain today and I will be wet.

Be ahead of the game, put that stuff on now, I think to myself.

Rain pants and jacket, probably the best investment I made!

Saturday April 6, 2002. Justus Creek: 2,550." Justus Mountain: 3,224'.

Here I am by the stream, with the sun setting low behind the Rhododendrons and pine. I am in heaven.

You get water. I don't. Big mistake!

Enough water to cook two pots of food and a little to drink during the next three miles to a shelter.

So, supper will be soup and noodles.

I use the orange shovel for the second time. Ah, the art of locating a spot with diggable soil and taking care of business.

Bedtime will come quickly, for my body needs to rest, in order to walk the eight miles tomorrow.

It takes me forever to pack the pack. Big yard sale...

And, did I mention, that I also have my monthly stuff to contend with.

If I make it through this week, with what I view as: "the inconveniences of life," then I'm good to go the distance!

Transitions...

You: in your crazy creek chair, sleeping bag around your waist and feet, green fleece jacket and woolen hat....leaning back and lighting a cigarette,........ as the sun sets and the first star of the night rests upon the horizon.

Sunday April 7, 2002 Gooch Mountain Shelter: 14.6 miles from Springer Mt.

7:43 P.M. finally reaching the shelter after five miles of walking with very little water.

I have a runny nose and I am two days into the week that messes up each month.

On approaching Justice Stream; water never looked so good to me!! The art of pumping water... I really like squatting by the stream and thinking. I pump two liters and, impulsively, decide to wash my hair. ...get it wet and soapy, rub my scalp, and get it wet again... right here in the mountain water! Then, using my big black all cotton *trucker- shirt* as a towel, I wrap my hair up to dry, before combing it out.

The shelter has a privy, how modern! Cooked dinner and when I was taking my stove apart, I dropped the fuel intake valve and it is now clogged with sand and you say, "Jesus D.! What are yah doin'?"

"Hey, I don't know. I'm *just,* not that good with this thing. What can I say?" I answer.

Now we are readying ourselves for another nights' sleep *on* the tarp, not *under* it. Banking it won't rain, I bet ten games of bowling on this nights' weather.

Here's how it goes: I pay for bowling games if it rains before four A.M. and you, if it doesn't. Well, as luck would have it, at about two A.M., the rain begins, a few drops at first, to fall upon my face. I hope it will stop. No, I *pray* it will stop. Neither of these mental efforts stop, what becomes a steady and soon torrential down pour. A river of rain finds its way into my bag, which is situated on a slightly sloping tent site.

I am wet and soon to be completely drenched, but don't care. I pull my pack under the grounded tarp. No time to ponder a bet now.

Where are my boots? …Glasses? …Headlamp?

Jesus Christ! There's a lot to lose at night! I am getting wetter and wetter. Okay, this isn't working. We must get under cover.

Scrambling now, we move with our pads, packs, and bags up to the pea stone floor porch area of the shelter, to finish off an interrupted sleep.

I'm out ten games of bowling! But, oh well, at least it assures me that bowling is in my future!

I awake to the smell of powdered eggs being cooked and a sea of legs above me.

Hikers getting ready to move out… Where are my glasses?

It is a little after ten now. Awake. I eat a few bars and granola with powdered milk. Plus, a bonus: uneaten powdered eggs!

All gear is excessively damp as we head on our way in the mist and rain. The woods smell so sweet and musty. We walk through a burned out section of forest, dwarfed by finger-like tree branches reaching upwards into a gray nothingness. …

Where is the sky today? Where will I find myself today? Who will I be at the end of the road?

Gooch Gap: 2,784' Big Cedar Mountain: 3,737' 21.0 miles from Springer, Mt.

My feet have a couple of hot spots on them which I've taken care of.

So, I missed writing on Wednesday…. But here's where I was:

Jarred Gap: 3,250', Wood's Hole Shelter: 26.6 from Springer, Mt. and Bird Gap: 3,650' 26.7 miles from Springer, Mt.

Just walking….

Blood Mountain: 4,461' 28.3 miles from Springer, Mt. Which, "according to tales of Creek and Cherokee Indians, a battle between two nations on the slopes of the mountain left so many dead and wounded that the ground ran red with blood, which inspired the name." [Appalachian Trail thru Hikers Companion. p.11]: 2002 Edition.

Blood Mountain is, also, the highest point on the Georgia A.T. and its two room stone shelter was built in the 1930's by the Civilian Conservation Corps.

Slaughter Gap: 27.4 miles from Springer, Mt.

Great day!

Kneels Gap: 3125' U.S. 19/129 Wallace -Yi Visitors Center.30.7 miles from Springer, Mt.

Stop for a bit.

Get a new bite valve for my water filtration system, pretzels, a bunch of bars, instant potatoes, and a cranberry juice.

Mountain Crossing of Frog Town Gap: Blairsville, Ga.

…sunny and warm… All my stuff is out, in true yard sale fashion and I'm sorting [out of habit] for laundry, but really everything is: *muddy, crusty, and sweaty*!

Take a shower.

You weigh your pack. I watch. Knowing mine is heavy, I just don't need the confirmation.

…my first call home…

To hear the voice of my daughter, saying, "I miss you, Mom." was quite comforting.

Mail a postcard. Check out the hiker box.

Use a regular bathroom, for what I envision will be one the last times ever, before walking through the famed archway.

Levelland Mountain: 3942' 32.2 miles from Springer, Mt.

We hike another couple of miles before ending the ten mile day, all the way from Woody Gap, Georgia.

You set up the tarp, which involves collecting leaves to anchor the plastic. I gather several flat stones and make a table for our stoves.

The fog is all around and you are, now, going for water.

It's eerie here, alone and I think *What if you don't come back? How far away is the water, anyway? You've been gone too long.* My comfort meter is falling…hmm…mm… *O.K…*

Finally, I hear your footsteps on the hillside and excitedly call out, "Hey, I started my own stove!"

Eat white Tuscan bean soup and go to bed, here on this thorny knoll somewhere along the trail.

Thursday April 11, 2002.

Walk about one mile to **Rock Spring Top, 33.5 miles from Springer, Mt.** then four miles crossing **Raven's Cliff, Cowrock**

Mt. 3842' 35.4 from Springer Mt., and Tesnatee Gap 3138' 36.2 from Springer, Mt., before reaching **Whitely Gap Shelter and Pearl Rock: 36.9 miles from Springer, Mt.**

Reach the shelter at 7:30 P.M. People are settled in for the night.

We get water and decide to continue on in the night using our headlamps. The night air is balmy. The path is relatively smooth. Walking at night is so peaceful.

We walk another mile, or less, until 10:30 P.M. and stop near **Hogpen Gap: 3450'37.1 from Springer, Mt.**

You set up the tarp. I get out my stove and begin to play with it 'cause it's not lighting.

Now, about the condition of my stove: As you know, I dropped it in the dirt several nights ago, didn't clean it right away and after several increasingly difficult lighting episodes those little grains of sand have bunched up and completely clogged the fuel intake valve.

And… if that isn't enough, to add to this dilemma… last night I inadvertently left it out in the rain! *So*, when I say: I *played* with my stove, that's exactly what I mean!

A little more fiddling and: *Voila!* Miraculously, the thing lights up, presenting me with a rather *large* blue flame, 'cause I let out a little to much fuel!

I make mashed potatoes with salt and the D spice mix. Great!!

Did I mention that I bet five games of bowling that it wouldn't rain last night?

And, you're right! I lost. I am now, out fifteen games of bowling!

…and, to comfort my burgeoning losing streak, tonight, I am betting two games of bowling and a cocktail! The rationale here is: that if I'm losing, a margarita will ease the pain, as well as, soften the blow to my smokin' credit card.

How about this early morning rain? Somebody wants me to bowl! Or, drink! Or both! Total games out: twelve, plus, one cocktail. I guess I'm not that good at predicting weather either!

Ah, the silly things that make this hike so enjoyable.

So, a look at me…. my sleep has been restless, to say the least.

I wake, not being able to breathe. I want all this concern, in, and, with my life to cease.

This is an enriching process of unlearning, cleaning the slate, then, rebuilding.

I'm out here walking to find something, and that something, could just be…. me.

It is overcast as I peer out of the tarp. The rain is puddling on the blue.

I had a bad dream last night.

whose pain tore me from this sleeping bag slumber?
whose dream did I awake from on this fog filled floor?
with curtains drawn,
a chorus of animal eyes watch as I sleep
exposed
to slumbers   haunting holes

I need to call home.
I need to keep walking.
My feet have several blisters.
My hair is outta control!
My nose is sun burnt.
I am becoming happy.

Friday April 12, 2002

….under blue, feeling the shape of nature within, with all that I possess on my back or at my side.

a net of silk
dancing in the breeze
strong enough to withstand a single drop of rain

How will the shape of nature manifest itself in my next art piece?

I saw the color of my last painted nude in the setting of the sun.

Whose handy work was that? And where did he hide?

Saturday April 13, 2002 2 P.M. Unicoi Gap, Ga. 2949' 50.7 miles from Springer, Mt. "Unicoi Gap was first crossed by an old Indian Trail. Later, it was the route for the first road built across the mountain range. Until 1966 the trail from Unicoi Gap to Neels Gap was the longest section of the A.T. in Georgia not crossed by a paved road. It is now crossed by Georgia 75."[Appalachian Trail Guide to N. Carolina-Georgia, p.137]: 2002 11th Edition.

It is raining and we are huddled and bundled near and under the trail information sign. It is eightish.

We cook our dinner at the trail highway crossing. Tuscan Bean Soup, maybe…

Listening as the cars and trucks go by, we try to predict the makes of the vehicles by the sounds they make. A heightened awareness of the world around us perhaps…or just a simple, silly game to amuse ourselves with.

After dinner and our game, we pack up.

Headlamp secure across my forehead.

Snack bars in an accessible side pocket. We head out into the night.

I hear the owl again, which is a good sign.

Rocky Mountain: 4017' 52.0 miles from Springer, Mt.

Night hiking: A challenge to the psyche to say the least. This leaving home to hike the A.T. is all about a challenge.

You are ahead of me, maybe as much as a mile. My fear begins to rise. I call your name. You are out of my comfort range. I call out your name, again, soft at first, then louder… and louder still, ….which in turn, you call back, "D. are you alright?"

Of course I was… but, that animal instinct, to be safe from night predators, was taking over. My mind was telling me to find a safe shelter, yet my body was upright, walking with the weight of a pack and vulnerable to whatever the darkness held.

Once the night was fully set, it really didn't make any difference to me. It was just the encroaching darkness that messed with me.

How fast could I run to escape a predator?

I am pretty much thirsty and hungry all the time now, and I never know where I am…just following you on the trail!

So….If you don't know how you look on the outside, but you know how you feel on the inside, then the outside shall be as the inside. The two come together as one. The outside look, matches the inside feel.

Saturday April 13, 2002 2:30.

If I heard the sound… …of thoughts on painting

When I close my eyes, I see the verticalness of the trees, tipping to the right. In the painting, the newly textured, tree gnarling trunk of a line will no longer be called a line. It will have a new definition. It will be its own component. Maybe, that's where the writing will go: carved on the trunk like initials. Etched for all time. To grow as the piece does.

I want to see something new, every time I look at the composition. I will write over it again and again, so many times, that the script loses its origin and by virtue of this layering a new meaning will be created.

…new words… Syllables lost, new ones found, letters of the alphabet left alone, combined, then, blotted out.

Trying to figure out, both, what I want to say, and the overall visual expression of the piece.

The colors: an earthly green, brown mahogany, umber, venetian red, and putty.

This is my soul laid bare on the canvas.

I hope this piece will surprise me.

I am simply the vehicle for its creation: disconnected and out of control.

…alone in the forest at night… I dream. A dream of the colors, now vacant from my finger tips. I feel the papers texture. I blend the blues and oranges of sunset into life.

Maybe the paper should be rough around the edges. Tear the paper, for I am torn.

I smudge the ink on my finger to get the color. I touch the art.

Here's a random thought: *How did I get my great white hair?*

Sunday April 14, 2002 11:30. Indian Gap: 3113' 53.4 miles from Springer, Mt.

…crossed Tray Mountain Road… We camp somewhere near the Cheese Factory: "the site of a remote Mountain Farm operated by a transplanted New Englander in the early 19th century." [Appalachian Trail Guide to North Carolina-Georgia, p.129]: 2002.11th Edition.

Setting up in the morning to sleep… No need to hang a bear bag.

Hikers pass us by. They have become familiar enough with our schedule and do not disturb the sleeping: Night Hikers!

The trail journal name for us is: the nocturnal nudists!

You sleep. I write. I sleep.

I eat and go through my meager possessions. Yah, the whole yard sale thing!

I wait for you to awake.

Readying ourselves, we begin walking again around 5.

Well, let me talk about Sunday night. We hiked up… **Tray Mountain: 4430' 55.9 miles from Springer, Mt., then, on to Tray Mountain Shelter.56.2 miles from Springer, Mt.,**

…where you get water, and we meet up with Wade, again.

I tell the bowling story, which people are laughing about.

I say, "I'm now out seventeen games and a cocktail!"

Wade says, "You better stop betting."

I say, "What the heck!"

A guy named Ody, who owns a bar in Florida, says, "I'll give you a ride to town tomorrow. Just wait by my truck in the parking lot."

We have about thirteen miles to go to Hiawasee, Ga.

Leaving late in the afternoon we pass a Boy Scout Troop heading towards the shelter. Boy Scouts are notorious for bringing all the great junk food one long's for on the trail. They are, also, usually tired of carrying the weight of this junk food so, they are more than happy to stop and talk with a thru hiker and share their prized junk food. Boy Scout junk food pretty much looks like: Ring Dings, Devil Dogs, Twinkies... you get the idea, *right*?

We, or should I say, I gladly accept their offerings and safely stuff them in a side pocket. What's a few ounces when you're talking frosting! *Right?* So...o...o worth it!

...back to walking. It is raining and incredibly muddy.

The front- part of my upper legs, feel so weighty. But, this is not about giving in to minor discomfort.

We walk into the night. My early evening fear creeps in. Dusk is *so* hard for me.

We walk for quite a ways with no lights on at all. Eyes adjusting, we follow the now, etched and shadowed, umber- colored dirt path. ... ...just a line in the night.

I become fearful and haunting thoughts take over. I can't walk any faster. I don't want you too far ahead. This forty-five pound pack is weighing me down.

Your pee breaks give me time to catch up, but not time to rest.

It is raining. The mist leaves the forest feeling and looking so prehistoric.

Further along the way, at a pee break for you, I do manage to catch up.

You ask, "What's up D? How ya' doin'...?"

I answer, "I'm fine." But I'm not.

"I want this ring off my finger," I quietly say.

Stop.

"I've tried for two days now and it's not coming off," I continue.

You do not respond.

So here, right now, in the middle of Georgia, in its rain and mist-filled darkened forest at 7:30 ish, I stand, stopped. Pack off. I am twisting and turning and incrementally moving the gold band around my finger. ...Upwards now, and, towards the knuckle; feeling its abrasiveness upon my skin.

You wait. You are silent. No words spoken. Completely consumed and focused on the event at hand.

I am determined that this *will* be the spot where *it* comes off.

Stop.

Breathe.

I *feel* it give way. ...my heart races...

Stop.

A strange feeling of sadness compounds this emotional moment as I slip the ring past the swollen and irritated knuckle and off my finger!

Quiet.

...forest stillness

A single smooth medal band, now lays cradled in my palm.

Hush.

Silence.

You, uncommonly still. Waiting for me this time...

I am momentarily in a world of my own. ...alone... ...me on my own...

A tan line impression is all that remains. The shadow of a ring...

My headlamp, like a beacon, is shining upon this precious metal.

I turn towards you and say, "You should, maybe, take this ring now. I want to throw it away. I think I'll do it now!"

You say, "Don't. Just give it to me, D."

So, you take it and put it in your Nalgene bottle. I watch as it lands and mingles, now, amongst all the vitamins. Then I turn away

and stand, head back with arms outstretched towards the sky....
breathing in all the air; that is to be mine, for just... one long
moment.

And so it is that, in the stillness of night, high on the
Appalachian Trail, in the middle of the Georgia forest that I begin to
breathe again.

Here's to just being quiet in these woods.

I am free! Am I free?

From here we begin, again, to walk in the silence of a wooded
forest.

Still.

I lead for my light is already on, and I now have this huge
amount of adrenalin to unleash.

"Slow down," you suggest.

"Am I walkin' too fast?" I ask.

Then, I do slow down a bit. We continue on.

"Maybe we should stop for food and rest. Whaddaya think?"
you ask.

"Sure," I reply.

So we do.

A new home every night requires careful looking. The
requirements are: Soft ground, closeness to the trail, a good tree to
hang bear bags, and plenty of water.

We cook instant mashed potatoes and lentil soup. .. And, finish
with the Boy Scout goodies, eating the once coveted icing by the
finger full.... just *plain* right outta the can!

And, set up our "blue- house" tarp, now called: The Taj Mahal!

I learn to hang the bear bags. Now, there's an *art* to this, and
I've *kinda* watched you these past few nights, and *kinda* have the
basic idea so,… here's how it goes....

First, one has to find a good stone to wrap the rope around,
next find a good tree branch, then aim and *gently* toss the stone up
and *hope* it goes over the designated tree branch.

You are busy setting up the tarp as I toss the string- wrapped
stone up, up, up, …and then, I hear the stone land, which coincides

with a booming baritone voice yelling out, **"What The F…!! D, are you tryin' to kill me!"**

Scared, I run towards you and meekly ask, "Did I hit you?"

Just how mad at me are you? I think before I state, "I'm done. I can't do this."

Then we end up laughing so hard and so long….

Guess I'll stick to tarp set-up!

You then hang the bear bags and *I* hang out my trucker shirt, one purple sock and a purple washcloth.…more manageable activities and less likely to cause any injuries! We eat, we laugh and we swear a lot.

It rains and rains all through the night. My sleep is restless and wakeful. Every two hours I feel myself wanting for air. Am I wanting for life? …to *live?* Why can't I breathe at night?

This Sunday morning in the rain I write about the day to come. The sun did make a momentary appearance, brightening the forest floor and bringing with it a hope I hadn't felt in years.

Now, with water puddling and pouring off the roof of this house of blue, somewhere in the mountains of Georgia, and with birds calling and the forest floor just ready to burst forth with the life of spring, I sit. And wait; for *what?*

…Back to Art. I will carve the names of all the hikers I meet into the strong vertical of the tree. …In the middle. This experience, these people are the mural. All these eyes have helped me.

<u>Monday April 15, 2002. 9 A.M. Sassafras Gap, Deep Gap Shelter: 3550' 60.7 miles from Springer, Mt. Addis Gap: 3304' 61.5 miles from Springer Mt. to Kelly Knob: 4276' 62.6 miles from Springer Mt. Powell Mountain: 3850' 64.6 miles from Springer Mt.</u>

We are eating our dinner in the parking lot rest stop. …Too tired to hitch hike into Hiawasee. It is 10:30 P.M.

We hiked through the night again. I fell three times and bruised my elbow.

Sweating like crazy, through sweat glands I didn't even know existed!

My pack is heavy. It is wet.

I approach the time when I will make my second phone call home.

Ponderings: I have come back to the same place. The distraction is me. I am alone. I know nothing. I am dirty and sweaty. I've challenged myself some, but not enough, though. I have pushed, in hopes of finding the answer, but it isn't coming.

Do I even know the question anymore?

There is still too much fear in me to know how to proceed.

All the fun, all the weird stuff, is just a distraction. A diversion from the deeper soul searching, answer seeking, purpose of my existence.

It's time to come totally clean, to tell all, to tell someone.

Is that someone me?

Find me.

Then embrace the day!

I rest on a bed of pine needles, under the blue sun -patterned roof, and next to a heap of mud encrusted clothing from the last night.

I am hungry and thirsty.

…air and water…

I bandage these blistered toes in the sunlight. Nothing can compare to my nighttime sleep.

Sleep without rest, dream infused dark, unsettled at best. I am painless.

This journey…

These words are all I have to give.

love is fleeting, love is momentary,
love cannot be held any longer than the air in your lungs

I'm only a witness to the unfolding of a new balance.
Let life take the upper hand and throw a curve ball.

Let life be the simple art of taking hair from a brush.

Let life be the warmth beneath toes upon a sun drenched sleeping bag.

Let life be found in the comfort of words.

I'm cleaning the slate here. I will figure it out at some point, and then there will be something else to figure out. It'll never end. *You, know,* that whole continuum thing.

Hey, do a little philosophizing with me here. ...on *finding the answer*:

First define answer. Then define question.

Is there a question within an answer?

The words surrounding the answer are meaningless, because the answer becomes the question; therefore there is no answer at all.

The point being: Is the answer the reason or the result of the question?

.... answers to questions precipitate additional questions which will then require answering, and so it goes...

Okay, so we are standing by the highway about ready to hitch into town.

You spot a guy coming out of the woods. Pony-tailed and tall, he walks across the highway and drops his pack, takes a seat, lights up a cigarette, and leans his back against a road sign.

"Hey, you want to catch a ride into town with us and split a hotel room?" you call to him.

"Sure!" he calls back.

I am shocked. I am silent. That was quick. You didn't ask me. I am skeptical. He is a stranger. You don't share anything with strangers. I am uncomfortable with this.

And, we are now with this hiker. We get a ride into town.

I am, all the way, wondering, how is this all going to work out?

...too tired to care anymore...

Monday April 15, 2002 Hiawassee, Ga. 66.8 miles from Springer, Mt.

Monday afternoon 1:30: sitting in the rocking chair outside Mull's Motel.

The sign says: "Be Back Soon" How soon? When did you leave? We don't know. Time is irrelevant. We are wanting to be inside a room. We are not walking. Our shoes are off.

Finally, we gain admission to this two-bed motel room.

Get the bump box. Buy a phone card, note cards and stamps.

We split the motel room.

Eat at Johnny's Diner. …listened to the juke box… It is closing time and mid -afternoon… We tip well.

We now walk barefoot through town looking for flip-flops; anything to give our feet a break. We find some at Rite-Aid.

Back at the motel…. and in the true spirit of weirdness, I wash twenty-one socks in the bathtub! …and hang them on the bear rope inside the hotel room.

We take showers. …an amazing amount of dirt. The bathroom is disgusting.

"Let's go bowling!" I say.

We hitch hike to a bowling alley in Bryarsville.

Upon arrival the owner tells us, "It's league night till 9:30 and then we close."

Bowling: Bowling is pretty big down south and leagues pretty much dominate the week. I am so sick of leaguers that I think I might *join a league*, just so I can bowl!

Clearly disappointed, we head back outside and begin our hitch hike back to Hiawasee.

You say, "Yah know, we'd have better luck, if you'd do the hitchin,' cars will stop for a girl."

"Okay, what the heck…" I say.

So, with thumb out, and you guys sitting there, I'm hitch hiking. Locals honk their horns at us. We wave. We laugh.

Then a cop drives by. He looks our way. He slows down. He turns around. He drives by us again. He stops. This local cop seems like he is ready for action and we are *it* for him tonight.

"Oh great, we're screwed!" you say.

He officially begins with the whole, "You know it's illegal to hitch hike?" thing.

"Yes," you answer.

He points and instructs, "Get in the car."

We obediently oblige.

The doors lock. I am scared and quiet. It's a cop car. I've never had a reason to be in a cop car before, but here I am, in his back seat!

The divider window is open a bit. A bullet proof vest is nestled between you and me on the back seat.

I am thinking, *we are going to jail for hitch hiking. How would I explain this back home?*

"Where are you going?" he continues.

"We are A.T. thru hikers and we just wanted to go bowling but it was league night so we couldn't bowl and now we are just trying to get back to our hotel," you, without taking a breath, reply.

"A.T. hikers? Where ya from?" he asks.

I answer, "Vermont."

Continuing on and subsequently realizing that we posed no real threat to his county he kindly says, "Well, here's what I can do. I can take you to the county line or the police station?"

We look at each other and you politely and clearly state, "The county line is alright with us officer."

You hear Guns and Roses: "Sweet Child of Mine" playing on his CD player and say,

"I like your choice of music."

"You like Guns and Roses?" he responds and turns it up!

Now I'm thinking: *life is getting better, here, in the back seat of this cop car in Georgia and, will be even better, when we reach the county line, and are let out!*

Ah….the county line! He stops. We exit.

We are walking; left of the lights.

A pizza parlor is across the street from us. We are hungry. Hikers are always hungry! But, it is closing time so, no pizza.

I am cautiously hitchhiking, again, despite the cop incident.

So…knowing that vehicles must stop an intersection, I explain, "My plan is to pray for a red light and then walk right over and ask for a ride."

"That's kinda brassy," you say. "But, go for it!"

"Okay" and with that, I watch the road and wait.

"How about I push the walk button?" you ask.

"Sure, go for it," I answer.

"Here comes one!" I call over in an adrenalin heightened pitch.

Your finger depresses the button.

The light turns red and the unsuspecting driver stops his truck.

His window is down.

"Here goes," I whisper to myself.

I walk right over and say, "Hi, we are A.T. Thru Hikers and are wondering if you could give us a lift to Hiawassee?"

He says, "Sure."

"Wow! That was easy!" I think to myself, as I turn and call out,

"C'mon guys. I got us a ride!"

I reluctantly ride up front and you two ride in the truck bed. I am nervous. I am scared. Yet I confidently start the conversation with, "Where's a good place to eat this time of night?"

He drops us off at a Mexican restaurant in Hiawassee at 11:30 P.M.

Tuesday April 16, 2002

We order several pitchers of beer and eat what appears to look like a Shoney's buffet once all our ordered food arrives. An hour or so later, our stomachs now satisfied, we pay, tip well and leave.

Wanting to play cards and not owning any I spot a Holiday Inn and say, "C'mon, hotels *must* have cards." So, off we go, right up the hill. I walk inside *and*, pretending to be a guest, I approach the front desk and ask, "Do you have a deck of cards I might borrow for the evening?"

"No," replies the receptionist.

Not taking her no-of- an -answer, I continue, "Are you *sure* you don't have any kickin' around somewhere?"

"No, I don't," she assures me.

I leave and meet back up with you. We walk down the hill and sit in the Gazebo. The dogwood is in bloom. ...Azaleas, creeping phlox.

...back in the motel room. I really, really want to play cards. I notice that the owners are still up. I leave the room and knock on their screen door. They look up.

I ask, "Do you by any chance have a deck of cards I could borrow for the night?"

She says, "Yes" and hands me a deck.

"Thank you," I politely say.

We play the geography game, then poker.

Hey, it's just us, it's all our money.

You sleep on the bed. I sleep on the floor. Check out time is 11:30.

Wednesday April 17, 2002

...Socks, no longer on the bear rope but, now drying on the rocking chairs in the 70 degree plus Georgia sun in the parking lot of Mulls Motel.

This morning I will pack a bump box and mail it to Fontana Dam, N.C. and mail some stuff home. Even though I've reduced my pack weight by five lbs., the food I just bought feels like it keeps it the same weight.

Dill's Food City: instant potatoes, batteries, bars, bananas, baby carrots, noodles, hair tie, zip lock bags, bagels and cheese.

Postcard Home:

I am missing seeing you I will be home soon. The hiking is so awesome. Very hard work- I climbed up 1100' the other day and was so sweaty. I sleep under a tarp every night. I've hiked at night using a headlamp. The forest looks very prehistoric at night, with all the mist and dark shadows of the trees. Philosopher saw an owl. I scared a bird of some sort the other night. I am in Hiawasee now. Ate ice cream, [2 scoops of chocolate chip cookie dough] grilled cheese with every vegetable they had on it, French fries, O.J. Then later went out for Mexican food. I will be heading back to the trail later this morning-[Tues A.M.] Hope your vacation is great. I love you.

Had big dreams last night, breathing- *searching for air in the night..*

You have the crystal I gave you, before I knew I would be on this walk. I look at it and feel its color between my fingers…. Amethyst is my color.

Rocks are my game; the feel, the transparency, the edges, the shape… It came from something larger, much as I feel about myself, especially hiking at night. I am small, but part of something larger. I may never find out or I may learn tomorrow. How much or how little is of no consequence, once I leave this parking lot.

Noisy cars…shop front antique- selling - vendor- like- windows beckon me closer for a look. …At what?

Like a dream at 1 A. M. silent shopping, no entering here, no exchange of coins, no want for anything finer than what I can carry on this back.

Wednesday April 17, 2002

We meet Jester. He's rather tall, which is an under statement, because this guy is, a giant among us at way over six feet! We talk briefly, as he is just entering town and on his way from the post office with a bump box.

We are getting ready to leave Hiawassee.

Just before Ashtray enters the trading post, he kiddingly calls out, "Hey, there's a white limo and it's our ride."

"Uh, huh, sure it is," I half heartedly reply.

While Ashtray is inside this guy walks towards us and says, "Hi. How yah doing?

"Good," we nonchalantly answer.

"Where are you from?"

"Vermont"

"Do you need a ride anywhere?"

"Well, actually we do," we answer.

"Would you like a ride to the trail head?" he asks.

My thoughts here are: *hey, score! A ride without hitch hiking!*

"Okay," we answer, and in the same breath, ask the next question, "*So,* where is your car"?

"Over there," he says and points in the general direction of the parking lot. Not really sure of where he is pointing we ask again for clarification, "which car?"

"The white one," he answers.

"No way!" comes' an excited tandem reply.

When Ashtray comes out of the trading post, we tell him that we have a ride to the trail head.

He asks, "Where? …and, with who?"

Our fingers simultaneously point to the white limo! …Ashtray smiles… And, if he was thinking: *I told ya so,* he wasn't going to let it roll off his lips right then…anyway.

My first limo ride! …Packs in the trunk. We take our places on the plush upholstery.

Patsy Cline is singin' "Crazy", which brings a whole new meaning to both, being in the south and being a long distance hiker.

Interiors: polished dark wood, white leather seats, full bar, television. A rather luxurious ride for three, although showered, still sweetly- scented hikers.

How cool is this! A limo ride to the trailhead… Life doesn't get much better than this!

At the trailhead we take a bunch of pictures and…..

Dick's Creek Gap: 2675' 66.8 miles from Springer Mountain, Ga.

With packs secured to our bodies we enter the woods once again. It is 75 degrees. My pack is laden with food and I am full from town food.

Postcard Home: *The rain has held us up some. But, today is sunny and warm. We are headed out of Hiawassee, Georgia to Plum Orchard Gap Shelter. We are 96 miles to Fontana Dam N. Carolina which I think is another food drop and less than 10 miles to the state line.* **Rich Cove Gap** *and* **Bly Gap [3880'], Blue Ridge Gap [3020']** *a lot of gaps!* **Muskrat Creek Shelter [4600']** *Most of the time there is water every 2-4 miles. Pumping it takes about a 1/2 hour and we do this depending on the elevation 2-3 times a day. The weather is hot and sunny today. I have poison ivy now. I'll be out 6-8 days from the date of this letter. Will go over* **Standing Indian Mountain [5498'],** *look this up on the internet. A guy has a digital camera and is going to make a hiker website.*

We hope to hike 11 miles today. We will not go through any towns again until we reach Franklin, N. Carolina. I love you all and miss you.

Just before Bly Gap we cross the North Carolina/Georgia State Line. We stop. I touch the carved wooden sign and you take a picture. …An emotional moment for me and, the first milestone of this journey.

I am walking slow, sweating like crazy, but making it none - the -less. I feel energyless and fall behind, which only frustrates me. I am just not able to catch up. *And*, for every catch -your-breath switch back, there is a looming long up.

I think to myself: *just set your pace, and keep it. Think about something else and soon you'll be done with this up. ...blah...blah...blah.... and yah...so, the mental plan worked! I made it!*

Once on top I drop the weight of my pack...breathe... and stretch these, now, sun -browned arms open wide, for whatever wants to enter their space. ...My sweaty space.

...My energy space. ...My core.

I eat a bunch of snacks. Drink the lemonade-cranberry drink which, I suspect is not helping me. Pure sugar, not the necessary replacement fluid my body really needs. Rest over. Pack back on.

We continue on for a couple of miles. I feel dizzy and like I'm walkin' in a fog. Reluctantly I say, "I'm not sure I can continue tonight.

I've only walked four miles and I'm not happy. I don't think I can press on."

Recognizing my genuine inability to continue, you agree to stop, then, say, "Let's get water and go to the shelter."

I eat a bagel and unroll my bag and go to bed. I fall asleep to the smell of incense and the crackling of a camp fire. ...voices about. I dream. ...Dreams not to be recalled.

Thursday April 18, 2002.

Now, it is morning. ...Thirsty. I *must* drink a whole lot of water before starting out. ...Hungry. I must eat a bunch, for I didn't really have any supper.

"I Am Hungry!" I say right out loud. I have a bagel with peanut butter, dried apples, and a Cliff Bar. *This oughta do it!* I drink almost a liter of water.

When I finish writing I will go to the stream to wash my face, brush my teeth and fill my Nalgene bottle. Did I mention that I like pumping water! Although, I'm finding out that my pump is not really the best.

Well, perhaps it would be okay for a day hiker, but it is definitely not efficient enough for a thru hiker...'cause it's taking me *forever* to fill my bottle!

I must be able to do this walk....

There is poison ivy *everywhere* in these woods, mosquitoes abound, and lots of wildflowers.

Trout lily, skunk cabbage, vetch, violets, spring beauties, mint, dogwood, wild cherry, birds…. and of course, majestic mountains…

…random conversational sound bites…

*Micky One Sock: "I'm a retired high school principal. I've been a principal for 30 years. I've got a wife who works. I'm retired, now, and can hike for months."

*"My body needs food. I feel it. But my body or better yet my stomach isn't big enough."

*"Descartes: a philosopher: check it out."

*"if you think for yourself you probably wouldn't be in half of the situations that you are put in…"

*VQ: "I'm a night nurse hiking alone, although one is never truly alone out here. I quit my job in Massachusetts and plan to hike the whole trail."

…there is water every two miles

"I don't think I'm going to pump any," our hiking companion matter -of- factly states.

"Why?" I ask.

"Because I have water purification tablets," he says.

"What the heck are those?" I ask.

You explain that they save time and energy, but I'm not convinced and will stick to pumping what I need to get me through each 2 mile section.

So, my hair is down. I want to cut it. The trail is no place for high maintenance hair, which mine isn't really, but even the task of braiding and tying it up is becoming more effort than I care to expend.

…Coffee in the morning. …Getting water.

…more randomness

*Steve: Bob Dylan says, "Beck is the only music worth listening to these days."

*Big Wu: "Tracking Buffalo through the Bathtub."

*"The greatest songs ever written have three chords: three chords and the truth." Bob Dylan."

Thursday April 18, 2002 5:24 P.M. Bly Gap: 3880' 75.6 miles from Springer Mountain, Ga.

...Beautiful day. I feel great! Eight miles to Standing Indian...

...To prepare for a walk in the night...

...To long, for rest in the early morning hours.

...To sleep through the night, only to wake. *What do you think about when walking through the woods?* No answer. No words spoken.

So, walkin' along, I'm still trying to figure out the night breathing thing. And, it comes to me, that, my nights rest just happens to be the lowest part of my day.

All day long I am busy, distracting myself with walking, pumping water, cooking, basically anything that comes along or strikes my fancy. I work hard, climbing. I sweat. I think. I am my own experience. I am reaching inside my core. Then comes the night and with it an uncontrollable darkness where every dream is free to roam, every bodily movement uncalculated, every rapid eye movement, its own impulse. I slip into this free -state unaware of its future. I know nothing of these dreams, of these twists and turns in the dark of the night.

This sleep is the downward spiral of my daily existence. I am within a fraction of death. Then, I gasp, breathe in the life sustaining air and reenter the night. This is the ebb of my existence. This is as close to death as I shall be for now. I am me. I am it. I am.

...Feeling healthy. Maybe that's why I reach for the sky in the photos you take of me. I am giving myself to the clouds....to the mountains. I am connecting with something larger than me. I am nothing. I am but a speck on the face of the Earth.

Somewhere in here, Ashtray runs out of cigarettes and leaves us to satisfy an urge greater than one can imagine.

And…. no one knows it, but I am carrying a pack of Camels. *Now* is not the time to give them up, though.

Friday April 19, 2002. A.M., Deep Gap: 4340' 82 miles from Springer Mtn, Ga.

Four more miles to go to complete this 10-11 mile stretch of walking. The owl is calling. We hike through the night.

Sleep is on the tarp in the parking lot.

…The moon but a sliver. …The stars. …The lights of the surrounding towns.

Awake at 8:58 A.M. peanut butter, Swiss cheese, baby carrots and peanuts. Going up an1100' foot rise today to **Standing Indian Mountain: 5498', which is 84.8 miles from Springer Mtn. Ga.** The best view! It feels like home to me.

"Standing Indian Mountain is the highest point on the trail south of the Great Smokies." p. 19 [Appalachian Trail Thru Hikers Companion, 2004]

I hope to get in 15 miles with breaks and…

cradled in slumber
a breathless sleep
unravels old sorrows

What is this all about? …These feelings. What if I were to connect with another artist at this very moment? Would the creative response be explosive?

I think. I think. I think I am becoming closer to the source of my creativity. I feel something that has been unknown to me: a sense of creative perspective. From these woods comes that, which has passed by my door many times over, a creative resource…

Friday, April 19, 2002: Albert Mountain: 5220' 97.1 miles from Springer Mtn., Ga.

I am overwhelmed by this mountainous scene. ...the blues, new-leaf green and burgundy.

Albert is my challenge. ...Very steep and rocky. Nearing the peak, I pause on the shear rock outcropping.

I scan the barren landscape for a hand hold, and a secure place for my poles to anchor the next step.

No good place to grab onto anything. I can't figure it out. I must trust my next step will work, or risk falling.

Calculate and take the chance.

I'm so far away from help should anything happen. I'm stressing. I am alone.

Eyes water, then quickly dry as you call: "D, are you okay?"

"Yes," I coolly answer, hoping you won't detect my fear.

I think to myself, *c'mon, you gotta move.* **Now!** *Go. I don't know if I can stretch my legs that far, but. [Deep breath]...with 40 pounds on my back and poles clasped tight under my arm, I spring across the ledge and land safely, exclaiming to anyone within earshot: "I DID IT!" ...and the walk continues.*

What could *possibly* make a difference? ...This life of mine. ...This struggle.

This seemingly endless search...is painful at times. I am trying. I am inching myself forward. I am alone. ...Always. My sadness is my artistic expression. ...For all who choose to look. Sometimes, I feel like: Today, now, thirteen miles from Standing Indian Mountain, and finally on top of Albert Mountain that: confronting inner turmoil head on is a huge price to pay for any color I may commit to paper.

Okay, that said or thought, time to continue on with the task at hand.

like a wisp of a cloud
I am about to slip into a world
that once had no room for me

The Albert Mountain Fire Tower: 5220'

It is one of the few remaining fire towers. No water. We climb its metal steps. The mid day clear 360 degree view is amazing. The viewing platform is closed, but *you* are not to be deterred by a lock!

"C'mon," you say, "Lets go up"

"Whaddaya mean *go up?* It's locked," I reply

"You can just climb up on the outside, like this," and with that said, off you go… and, although I am strongly discouraging you not to continue, you are at this point, unstoppable, … and all I can do is watch this death defying exhibition of gymnastic talent and take as many pictures I can, 'cause if you die here, then at least there's documentation of you enjoying yourself right up to the final breath!

As for me, if you fall and die my circumstances will become quite different. I will be alone, all alone, out here in the middle of freakin' nowhere, all by myself. Maybe I should have joined in on this escapade of yours to spare myself all this contemplation.

All these thoughts, clouding my mind, soon vanish as you reclaim your space on the concrete landing near me.

I need to write. You wait.

Friday, April 19, 2002 Big Spring Shelter, 97.7 miles from Springer; Rock Gap Shelter, 103.0 miles from Springer; Wallace Gap: 3720' 103.7 miles from Springer

We are six miles beyond Albert Mountain and 103.8 miles from Georgia. We walk tonight til 11:30 P.M. before setting up camp. We sleep in the Palace Hotel Ballroom, as it is now called.

Saturday, April 20, 2002.

…Awakening. The sun is shining on this hillside.

You are such a good sleeper.

Hoorah for me! Finally, I'm up six games 'cause I bet that I wouldn't move from my spot in the night and I didn't.

<u>Note:</u> I tend to move a lot in the night, so this is a major accomplishment for me. I have been known to take over the entire tarp floor space. I even bent a hiking pole in the process once. I had to really, really, concentrate before sleeping on *not moving.*

Bowling and cocktails are bigger motivators than I ever could have imagined!

So tired… I want a shower, a good breakfast, to do laundry. Cut my hair.

Get my food drop, and get on with it…

…as I go through the A.M. routine, I'm thinking, *I'll buy some bread, several bottles of good whiskey, nail clippers and tweezers, some Camel Lights, band aides, and a big - ass short sleeved tee- shirt and a lighter. I want to go bowling. You are now up 24 games (due to my poor weather predictions!) plus a cocktail compared to my four games and a double cocktail. A Long Island iced tea, or Tanquaray and Tonic. Margaritas! Whatever…all, with a shot on the side!*

It was so good to eat and sleep last night. I did not do my dishes, though. Big mistake! As I retrieve my bag from the bear bag line, I think *this ought to be sweet today, to look at that cooked - on -food- mess- of -a -pot. I'm a freakin' domestic misfit out here! But, hey, this is my thing for now, and I really only have me to answer to!*

Winding Stair Gap, U.S. 64: 10 miles from Franklin, N.C. 106.8 miles from Springer

See white trillium and jack-in-the pulpit.

We hitch a ride into Franklin, N.C., which proves to be fairly easy. Get a ride to the Haven Motel, where we will spend the night. We drop off our stuff and then go to the Post Office, show our ID's and, retrieve our precious food.

The owner of the Haven Motel gives me and two other hikers a ride to the outfitters.

This is where I meet Gourmet Dan. Yep, right in the back of a pick up 'cause nobody in their right mind would want a bunch of smelly hikers inside their truck! At the outfitters I have my picture taken for the hiker wall.

I buy black shorts and *finally* a cool max t- shirt, a compression sack, and a Pur water filter. I just love trying on clothes!

On our way back to the motel we stop at Kentucky Fried Chicken, whereupon

Gourmet and this other guy, order the largest freakin' bucket of fried chicken I have ever seen, complete with coleslaw and rolls and jumbo drinks! *And,* in true hiker fashion this food is completely devoured before we get back to the motel!

At the motel I take a shower and you order a pizza.

From the motel window we notice a pick up truck with a bunch of hikers in the back and one of them just happens to be Ashtray.

"Hey. Hi. Guess you found your cigarettes?" I say and continue with, "are you headin' out, now? Do you want to split the room with us and stay one more night?"

Sounds kinda familiar, doesn't it?

…and knowing fully well, that our one nights usually turn into two or three, you, in between a drag say, "Sure." ….and once again, we are three.

That settled; I proceed to do all my laundry in the sink and hang it out to dry on the rocking chairs outside the room.

Next, on the mental list of things to do, is to go to the local grocery store and buy: bananas, red delicious apples, baby carrots, raisins, fritos, cheese, cranberry juice, and chocolates for my food bag.

While I am shopping, you jam with the owners in the motel office.

Guitar and banjo playin' <u>Rocky Top…</u>

"Hey! That song never sounded so good," I say, upon returning with my food supply.

A few beers later and back in the room. I need to rest.

You go out and return with all the makings for Long Island Ice Teas and hair dye.

...ah …*hair-dye*…

"You want to dye your hair?" you ask me.

"Uh, huh, sure, whatever," I reluctantly reply. Then you begin to braid my hair. Next, the red hair dye goes on. I wait. …and hope this isn't going to be my worst nightmare! …and think: *how many washes did that fine print say?*

I come out of the shower.

"Can't tell a thing," I say, but as my hair dries in the 80 degree heat, I hear you excitedly exclaim, "It's awesome, D. You got Tie-Dye Hair!!"

"Great! Just what I was goin' for" … and then think to myself: *really, now, it isn't half bad. I can live with this.*

…. So, now, with the success of my hair, you dye yours.

"This calls for a toast! When are you gonna make those drinks?" I ask.

Yah, those tasty Long Island Ice Teas, of which I don't really remember the recipe, so I, confidently say, "A shot of everything and some ice! That oughta do it."

You generously oblige prior to an exuberant "Here's to tie - dye hair!!" toast.

Now it's off to Franklin Lanes, hitch hiking, of course and a little bowling.

Dinner consists of a salad, cheese, Fritos, onion dip, bagels, and a rum and coke.

I want to go to Ruby Rock Museum tomorrow. In town one day and I'm talking like a tourist. What's that all about?

so free to delve
so lax to retreat
amidst the dark
and everlasting night
life:
a heart beat into a dream
left
to roam

I call home. No answer. I leave a message.

I must go to the outfitters tomorrow to return the compression sack. I buy two Clif Bars and silver earrings.

At night we play poker which is a joke because I don't know how to play. We are laughing.

It's well after midnight and probably closer to two when you ask, "Do you want to take a walk?"

"Okay," I reply. You pack the stove and jiffy pop. We head out in the still of the night to the gazebo in the little park in the center of town. The moon is out, it is cold. Cops are on the prowl and we are likely suspects. They do not bother us.

I guess making popcorn on a whisperlite in the park is not a felony tonight! We eat and walk home.

Quietly entering the motel room, we two, fall in line and sleep.

Brother Paul: "Does this way of thinking keep you from getting hurt?"

Feeling pain? Does it keep you away? Keep you safe?

A thought… Every day I feel sadness, so deep, in my soul that all the words, in all the readings, and on all the paths, can't keep me safe. It is simple. This energy, this surrounding oneself with the words of another, and thinking, *that which keeps you safe, prevents me from being safe.*

I am ageless. I am just born. I know nothing. This experience harbors my fear.

It won't let loose my fear. It is mine, right so, to let loose. Yet, I guard it and even protect it. I think, I can't let it go. For, I will be empty. I have had this with me for so long. I don't know or trust how my body will react without it. Much like an alcoholic… I want to quit, but how? This is about the essence, the core of existence.

Why do I think that what I need is not already inside myself? What is it that I can't get from myself? Will I be forever seeking? Will I be forever on an avenue of escape? I am so fearful of life at times and so afraid to move from this false comfort zone.

You watch me unfold. You watch me iron out the wrinkles. You watch my soul unravel.

Exhale… Air escaping lungs…. A single breath leaves. . . I *can* change this tide, this tide that turns me over and over and over again.

I am out on this precipice alone.

Question: Is this why I stay up at night, play hard, walk hard, draw for hours on end, laugh with my whole body, cry with my whole body?

Night: When the lights go out. I am one and I face my oneness.

Touched by the wave that tossed me out… I am newly learning to swim, in order not to drown. When will I feel comfort?

Tears fall and gently rest upon my cheek.

How did it come to pass that falsehoods could lead me here, to these woods?

Hmm…m… Where am I going with this?

Ah, yes! Everything happens for a reason and this is the reason. This time, right now, is to think, to write and to shed some of that mind clogging debris.

Within the shelter of a lean-to, this solitude is its reward *and* the answer is as clear as the carved timber which holds me.

I am both mystified and oddly content.

…and, this is me, slogging through my baggage, trying to make some sense of it all…

Forty-eight hours in Franklin, North Carolina and we've yet to go to the Ruby Rock Museum. I'm really having a touristy moment with that ole museum. I *do* like rocks though, so that must have something to do with it!

"Driving into Spring…"

Ashtray sleeps on the floor with all his stuff in various stages of disarray: snickers, bags of mac and cheese, cigarettes, a lighter or two, fuel, sleeping pad, a Pepsi bottle, crusty socks and boots.

And this is where I write down his home phone number.

Sunday April 21, 2002. Swinging Lick Gap, 107.9 miles from Springer; Panther Gap, 108.8 miles from Springer; on past Siler Bald Shelter,: 4700' and Siler Bald.110.5 miles from Springer.

We hike out of Franklin at 4 P.M. "The highest point is Siler Bald (5216') named for William Siler, whose great grandson, the Rev. Rufus Morgan helped establish the A.T. in North Carolina." [A.T. North Carolina- Georgia, p.99]

I hike fast 'cause it's getting dark. I get to the field and wait. I don't hear your voice.

I call your name.

No reply. I *just* wait, as I am unsure of which way to go. I don't have the Data Book.

Impatient yet trusting my instincts, I slowly begin to climb up across the field.

The sun is setting.

I turn around and see you at the foot of the field. "C'mon," I call, "this is amazing!"

You heed the call and we summit nearly together.

"This is the most amazing sunset I've ever seen!" I say again.

"Hurry, or you're gonna miss it," I call out to Ashtray, "and we need to use your phone!"

Dialing the phone, you call Randy in California. We take turns talking and describe the setting sun until the charge runs out.

You shoot a whole roll of color film.

We eat as the sun sinks below the distant mountain then, gather up our stuff and hike over **Wayah Gap: 4130' 107.9 miles from Springer and Wine Spring Bald, 116.9 miles from Springer.**

This takes us 'til about midnight.

Tired we set up the tarp, hang the food and go to bed. The wind is howling. Lying beneath these bigger- than -life, bending - trees in the night, and I hope, I pray, that they will retain their branches, while our meager form of protection from the elements is billowing… it rains pretty much all night.

Ashtray utters the words, "*magic memories,*" in his sleep.

I say, *"What?"* And, then figure it out…

Upon waking we find that the tarp is heavily puddled. I mean, to the point where it is resting right on me like a giant blue water balloon! Ashtray pushes up on the tarp and before I can say, "What the"… the accumulated rain water rolls off and streams in on the uphill side of the ground cloth. *Move… Now!*

Not much is dry now, and to make matters worse, I am thinking *that I lost the bowling bet!* I'm stressing over a silly bet, at a time, when pretty much there isn't a piece of dry gear to be found! I mean really, I must get my priorities straight! Then I hear you say, "We didn't bet, D, so relax!"

...a very cold A.M., it's in the 40's. Wind chill: not going there. It's just freezing cold and all my stuff is on. I walk fast to warm up.

Monday, April 22, 2002 Wayah Bald Mountain Stone Observation Tower: Elevation: 5342' feet.

Postcard Home:

Monday @ Wayah Bald Mountain: Elevation 5200' or thereabouts. The explorer Desoto passed through here in 1540 in quest for gold. I can see Albert Mountain Fire Tower-10 miles away at least and Siler Bald Mtn. is where we were last night for the sunset.

And now here, where from the fire tower we can look off and see the Smoky! In a few days I'll be in the Smoky Mountain National Forest. We will have to stay in shelters-no tarping-because of the bear population. The shelters have screens on them to keep out bears. I won't be hiking alone as I often have been. We are hiking with a guy from Massachusetts. We are a totally compatible trio. Hope all is well at home. I miss seeing everyone. I'll be home soon. And I'll call when I'm in the next town.

We are able to see the Smoky Mountains from here and it's where we are going.

Havin' a little lunch… Two Astrophysicists' from Texas and a Black Lab…

Our companion whips up a concoction that will not likely be revisited in the future.

"It's a Trail Shake," he states.

Curious, now, I ask, "What's in it?"

"Just put a banana, water, and instant mashed potatoes in a Nalgene and shake!" he proudly explains.

"I am so glad that stuff is not in my Nalgene," I sarcastically say and continue with, "it just looks so nasty!"

Postcard Home:

We are camping under a tarp near the highway where the A.T. crosses 10 miles north of Franklin, N.C. USFS 69 We hiked 12 miles at least-from 12:30 Friday to about 11 at night. I was so tired it was hard to even think of cooking my food let alone hang the bear bag. There aren't too many trees with good hanging branches where we are. I have poison ivy on my feet, my nails are dirty, I may cut my hair in town today! It is just too much to deal with out here. My water filter is not cut out for this type of trip so at the next outdoor center I'm going to get an Insta Pure, but for now I am using a friend's. We climbed up Albert Mountain 5200' which was the most challenging rock climb. I was crying. It was so hard and I was afraid of falling. But the view was as overwhelming as the climb. We went up the fire tower and all around as far as the eye could see were mountains. The Smokies are to the north where we will be heading. …Truly inspirational and beautiful… I miss you all-you are all in my thoughts and dreams. Take care. Hey my trail name is "The Mad Bowler"- I'll explain later….

We are trying to go 17 miles today to…

Wesser, North Carolina. U.S. 19, Nantahala River: 1740' 134.1 miles from Springer.

You want to be within 4 miles of Wesser for tomorrow. I am, now, thinking of going to Damascus, Va. But we'll see.

*Now, f*or my *trail name*... I had tried out a couple early on, but because of the in -town extreme bowling, Mad Bowler just seemed like the best fit. So, now my shelter journal entries include a bowling tip or two and often a reference to one of our in town bowling forays!

Wine Spring Shelter, 115 miles from Springer, Cold Spring Shelter: 4920' 122.6 miles from Springer.

A major feat... We walk 18.6 miles today. We hike all day from Cold Spring Shelter. What a hike! What a walk! We are within 1 mile of Wesser, the outfitters, and a restaurant! This is my longest stretch of solid walking. Just a string of hikers in the night...

Headlamps like beacons guide us, up and down another gap, another peak, it is all the same... walking...we keep checkin' in with each other.

"Are you *okay* to keep going?"... "How are you doin'?".... "Let's eat some more"...

"Let's stop and make some coffee" ..."Wait a minute"... I gotta pop a few more vitamins".... "Watch out for that root".... "It's slippery down here".... "Watch your step".... "You're doin' great!" and so it goes... This woodland conversation keeps us sufficiently distracted from blistered feet and tired backs.

"We're almost there," you call out, "about another mile" And finally, at the foot of this long down is our nights' destination and, without any hesitation we drop our packs, line up our bags in a neat row and sleep on this leaf padded hillside. No bear bag hanging for us tonight, no tarp set up, no cooking, we are just spent and, *I mean,* spent! I am so tired that I only get as far as unbuttoning my shorts, before I crawl inside my bag.

My sleep is peaceful. No dreams and no breathing issues tonight, just sleep. In the morning, all is well with me. I pump water and wash.

The sun is coming up, fanning a pattern upon my brow.

I see Solomon Seal and False Solomon Seal.

This is *so* good!

We find that the Rufus A. Morgan shelter is nearby and that we are less than one mile from Wesser, N. Carolina.

From the shelter comes a weekender woods guy who says he's gonna take a bath in the stream. He's sportin' a knife, as long as his thigh, strapped to his waist. I'm thinking *Deliverance* here, but keep it to myself…

it's your town
it's all yours
take me there
leave me
draw the chords
of the night

Tuesday, April 23, 2002 12:46.A.M. Nantahala: 134.1 miles from Springer.

What happens here?

Nantahala Outdoor Center Café: Breakfast ends at eleven which presents a problem 'cause I've been thinking breakfast food for awhile, now. Make the mental adjustment and order lunch. Baxter is here and tells us of walking by us in the early A.M.

Hikers are a curiosity. A woman approaches me and asks a multitude of questions. We talk for a short while. She seems quite sincere and quite possibly a good hugger, too! *And,* before I know it, the following words are softly coming out of my mouth, "Um, I have *kind of an um, unusual* request."

"What is it, dear?"

"Well…this is a little awkward, 'cause I hardly, even, know you, but, well…could I… could I have a hug?"

And instantly think: *Did I really say that?*

"Sure, dear," as she opens her arms to warmly accommodate my, rather unusual and somewhat random, by all accounts, request.

Now, *I am*, embarrassed, but must admit, I do *know* how to pick a good hugger!

Then, Ashtray, his arm slung over my shoulder, and I have our photo taken by a high school girl doing a project on hikers.

Today, I will reduce my pack load and get some lighter gear before I walk any further.

Night hiking: We came down almost 3000' feet last night.

…half- moon…rock ledges, miniature iris and my first Lady Slipper...

I'm feeling the color, in the shape of this protected flower. The pink to white to creamy -white -striations, then the green...I will use this…somehow…

Late afternoon, do some laundry, and then leave...

its mottled mosaic floor
beckons leather clad soles
onward
beneath a lime- hued canopy

Tuesday Afternoon, April 23, 2002.

Reflecting ….as I sit on a perch of rocks, overlooking the Fontana waters, sun on my back, muscles strong, and legs, still willing to work.

High as I am, happy as I can be….today, now, alone on these rocks and feeling more together than apart.

What to do about now being free, feeling free inside myself, despite myself. Where are you now? Let go of it all! Did I get what I came for?

Me…. outstretched arms, browned fingers, eyes seeing anew, the day, the rain, the light filled sky… just leave me… alone… in this state of, seemingly, uncanny alertness.

Pink Lady Slippers, Blueberries, Wild Strawberries, Mountain Laurel, Rhododendron, Wild Geranium, Lavender, Trillium.

We walk the ridge line towards Fontana.

Tuesday night: Grassy Gap: 3050', 137.2 miles from Springer; Cheoah Bald: 5062', 142.2 miles from Springer; Stecoah Gap: 3165', 147.7 miles from Springer; Walker Gap: 3450' 159.0 miles from Springer.

I want to stay out here.

Wednesday: 11 miles to Fontana. The essence of the mountain shape, forms, and shades of color, are imprinted, secured, and catalogued for their recall to paper.

I am the lake resting between the mountain sides. I am the valley floor who harbors these feet. I am patient. I can walk forever. I am happy. I am satisfied with the moment…the now.

My gait is swift as I walk ahead of you.

Fontana waters, unrippled, reflect an azure sky….

…something about the setting sun and the increase of adrenalin, to know the day is ending…. the walk along the ridge top. …Looking down on the water. ..and from dusk, bent blue, deep blue, mottled cuts in the mountainside rest like a fine velvet cushion…. coupled with the red-bronze setting of the sun…. Ah… this is *why* I came!

Well, no longer alone, you catch up to me.

"Man, you were really cookin' bowler!" exclaims Jester.

"No. Not really. I just found my stride," I say.

Anyway, you have a phone, so we call the number in the data book for a ride, give an approximate time when we will exit the woods, hang up and continue walking. It is becoming dark on our descent. Another long, never ending down…

So, where will I go? Any where I want. I follow the path on this what- ever trail and as it should be, it feels right. No ownership.

A future feeling, undetermined, can only be modified by circumstances, which may ultimately save it from its own undoing.

I eat. I sleep. I bathe. I read stories in the shelter journals. I wonder where these *trail name* people are. ...on the trail or in life... What is their reason for coming out here?

...butterflies in a tree, still high upon this hill, the lake and waterfront far below. *Will this down ever end!!* And, as quick as this thought comes and goes, we exit the woods!

Finally, the parking lot, public toilets, a vending machine and in a few minutes our ride to Fontana Village.

I throw my gear in the back. I'm so done with it!

We ask our driver, "Where can we get food and beer?"

"Well," he begins, "food would be a few miles outta town, and as far as the beer is concerned, this is a dry county."

"A dry, *what*?" I ask, as I've never heard of such a thing

"County, mam, and it means no alcohol sales within the county limits," he elaborates for my still unbelieving ears. And I'm thinkin' ....*what the hell am I going to have my pizza with? Where have I landed?*

The conversation also includes a little tidbit about a kid who shot out a few street lights last night, for fun. Just get me to the hotel! I am so done with my day!

But, not so done that I can't write a quick journal entry. The 5.9 miles we walked from the shelter to the road left us averaging two miles per hour. Not too bad. This turned out to be an eleven mile day! Fontana Inn... Food... Sleep.

Postcard Home:

We got in at 9:30 P.M. Fontana Inn Village. We are going to see the dam today. Hiked 11 miles yesterday... Poison Ivy pretty much gone... The mountains are amazing. Wild flowers incredible! We will be hiking in the Smokies this next week. Will call soon... I am getting quite a lot of writing done. So, that's good. I think of you often and every night. Talk with you soon.

Wednesday night: Once in the hotel, it's only a matter of minutes before the insides of our packs explode across the crisp white linen bed covers. The rest is a familiar town routine: a hot shower, washing sweaty black tee's and crusty smart wools in the bathtub and eating. Hmm…no take out at this hour, so, we cook what's left in our food bags on our camp stoves on the deck *because,* not only is this a dry county, but all the restaurants are closed and vending machines are pathetic!

Five of us share the space, 'cause it's just how we're used to sleepin'

I take a sauna [in the men's room no less!]

Organize some stuff. Bump boxes.

I am mailing the following extra weight home: a purple washcloth, hand knit woolen socks, the Leatherman AKA "the *Juicer,*" coins, a rock, a purple long sleeve check shirt, a t-shirt, 2 pair of hiking socks, black shorts, a broken carabiner, a purple bandana, and a guide to wilderness medicine. My pack already feels lighter!

From the standing room only balcony, I see a coyote! He is just cruisin' the parking lot looking for food, *I guess.*

My sink-washed laundry is almost dry and I'll do another shirt before we leave, whenever that is.….

Thursday I am hungry and looking forward to breakfast. I head on down to the buffet. Like a kid in a candy store, my plate holds more than my stomach can comfortably digest. I bring you back several plates heaped with fresh fruit, potatoes, bread and eggs. *And coffee!!*

Later in the day you ask, "Do you want to play cards?"

"Sure, I answer, but, *ah,* there's one minor complication."

"What's that?" you ask, looking at me rather curiously.

"Well, when we play cards, we drink beer and this, being a dry county, kinda puts a kink in the plan," I say and add, "But, let me think about it for a minute."

I do love a challenge and this dilemma sets me on a mission. "Hmm... with all the people vacationing here, someone must have alcohol!" I excitedly say, as I head out the door.

"Whaddaya doing?" "Where ya goin'?" "You can't just..." your words fade as I call back from down the hall, "I'm off to see what I can rustle up, I'll be back."

So, I take a walk around the complex.

I spot a family unloading their SUV and I walk right up and, barely pausing for a breath, I begin a friendly conversation, which just happens to include the "dry county" thing and how I'm a thru hiker and would really love to have a beer while playin' cards with my friends and if they could spare any I would greatly appreciate it.

"Sure, we can help you out," he says, then heads into the cabin and returns with two beers.

"Thank-you," I say. Inside I'm thinking: *SCORE!* I am excited beyond belief. I actually did it. I got beers!!

I walk in the hotel room and say, "Hey, you guys I got the beers!"

You look at me with that, *I don't even want to know from who, or how you got these,* and then Ashtray, whose done the math, interjects, " two beers, three of us, that ain't gonna go too far."

And with that comment, my adrenalin kicks in and I announce, "Okay. I'm outta here. I found some beer once, I can find it again!"

Well, as luck would have it...right in the hotel, walking down the hall are two guys heading my way with coolers. Simple math here: coolers might equal beer.

"Hi, how are you guys' doin'?" I ask.

"Fine, how are you?" they politely answer.

"Fine," I answer.

A few additional conversational pleasantries are exchanged before I get to my story and the heart of the matter.

"I'm an A.T. thru hiker and I'm wondering if you know where I might find a few beers in this dry county?"

"Well," they replied "we have a couple of bottles right here in the cooler, but if you want to come out to the trailer with us, we can give you a few more."

"Sure," I calmly answer, as I begin following them down the hall and out of the building to the trailer.

We're still chattin' away when one of the guys opens the back of the trailer.

Inside are several Harleys and beer: Cases of Beer! It seems that these two are vacationing beer distributors! And it isn't Bud, either! This is a freakin' jackpot! I'm thinking: *you're not even gonna believe this!*

So, tryin' to contain my, what is now a, mounting over-zealous sense of excitement and super adrenalin rush at this amazing hook up, I coolly answer, "yes," politely to the guys question of "Would a couple of six packs work for yah?"

I wrapped the six packs in a towel, 'cause this *is* a dry county, you know, and heaven forbid anyone *seein'* beer, or, for that matter, *drinkin'* the stuff! How high school is this! But, I guess I can get arrested or something for the public display of alcohol! I talk some more with these guys, thank them, again, and promptly return to my second floor hotel room.

Inside the room I unwrap the two six packs. "Voila"! I shout out excitedly.

"Yah, great," you coolly reply.

"C'mon, here, I got us beers," I say, sounding more like I'm covering myself for an unsavory deed.

"I can see that *now*, but I was watching the whole thing from the balcony and wasn't quite sure what the heck you were doing," you pointedly state.

"C'mon, whaddaya think I was doin'? You wanted beer and I was gettin' beer!" I curtly and with the wind, now, outta my sails, reply.

"*I don't know, D... two guys, a trailer,* you coulda been gettin' kidnapped or somethin'! and we were ready on the balcony to..." cutting you off, I blurt out, "*to what?*" and then I continue, "Ah, c'mon, now, I was *fine* and I'm *here* and I got the *beers* just like we wanted so, let's just open these freakin' cans and *play some cards!*"

We drink beer and play spades until 3:30 A.M.

Don't know what the day will hold and that's ok. I want to stay here if it's rainy and do the local thing: tour the dam, go to the outfitters, get a few things, but I'll see. I must pick up the mail drop.

Ashtray says, "I might be going to Merle Fest."

I'm thinkin': *what the heck is a Merle Fest?* Anyway, whatever it is, its a couple hours away, so, he'll be hitching and gone the weekend. Don't know how things will get coordinated for us to meet up again....

I call home today and ask if it is possible for me to continue hiking for another month.

...unconditional acceptance....

Life is a lot like bowling. It's all in how ya spin the ball.

Paper: I never thought that much about the value of paper before this. In my little journal, I use a section of paper each time I write. I write very small. So small, that, only I can read between the lines. What if I run out of paper? I'll just have to write even smaller! I have an idea! I will save a page in the middle of this journal, just in case I reach the end and still have something to say. Back-up, it's all about back-up!

later than 2:30.....

nighttime gambler

starlight

swept up in

a web of chaos

Do you know that this weekend will end?

I wrote the best paper. I got the grade, but all is not well for this soul. ...write the names, sing the song, and bury me deep in words... What's important as I sleep and as I dream?

Me. Here, on this trail, tampering with a fire.....afraid of getting burned....

I play too hard to come in from the rain. I play hard all day.

Yet, when all is said and done, I fall under the cover of darkness. It's just me between the sheets, cocooning with white linen and shedding a layer

Friday, April 26, 2002

Another buffet breakfast… I bring the usual heaping plates of fruit, eggs, potatoes, pastries, and copious quantities of coffee back to the room.

I feel tired and low today. I don't want to stop walking. I fear this ending, so I've upped my time.

I will stay out another month...to ride the wave, walk the walk, and to be…

….this feels like home to me,

….the trees, the wind, the challenges…

Closer doesn't amount to a row of beans in the scope of the whole garden…and the whole garden is out here.

Now, with that settled. What to do with the day? I think to myself…*Hmm. I know!* and blurt out, "Let's play mini golf!" which was met with a look from you of *where did that come from* and *how random, but…*

"Okay," you say, and it's off to the rec room to get clubs and balls.

We play a rousing game of mini golf with all our hiker friends.

If I didn't love bowling so much… well, let's not go there!

Anyway, what a great way to kill an afternoon!

I'll pack later….

You play the piano in the dance room at Fontana Village. The chords… The brassy vocals… …Alone… I dance around the room with arms outstretched.

I sweep a trail of colorless tears across the hardwood floor.

The urge to paint is ever present.

"Time After Time": "If you're lost, you can look, and you will find me, time after time…"[2]

I am the girl in the movie.

The woman who lets you pass through a dream, untouched, undone

It's okay to be me!

It's okay to want for more. …this feeling, now ungrounded … set free… it's me!

….in this simple state…. in this mistless night… dark… against time

You are awake and in the early morning hours we watch, "The Dark Day of the Crow." …Kind of a creepy movie. No, it *was* a creepy movie!

You step out on the deck and say, "Hey, come and look at these clouds."

I am soon on the balcony, as you continue to say, "Don't you think they are kind of Dali-like?"

"Hey, *anything* would look Dali-like after *that* movie!" I sarcastically reply then add, "but, you are right, they are *kinda* like something from a Dali painting."

You smoke an American Spirit.

We talk.

Later this morning or afternoon, we will go into the Smokies for a few days….

Friday, April 26, 2002

Leaving Fontana Village… Fontana Dam Shelter…. Bees… Little Tennessee River, Fontana Dam; southern boundary, **Great Smoky Mountains National Park[1800'] 163.5 miles from Springer.**

"Fontana Dam, part of the TVA system, was constructed on the Little Tennessee River during WW11 to furnish hydroelectric power. The dam is 480' high, the highest in the East and the 6th highest in the U. S." [Appalachian Trail Guide, Tennessee-North Carolina, p.200]

You sign the register and get a backcountry permit at the Fontana "Hilton," even though we don't plan on staying in a shelter.

All hikers are strongly advised to sleep in a chain-link fenced bear-proof shelter. I've, yet to see a bear, but the book says that, "between four and six hundred bears reside in the park."

The book, also says: *only thru hikers* are *permitted to tent-camp at shelters.* How fortunate! 'cause we're thru-hikers who like to sleep under a tarp!

Walking across the dam I meet motorcyclists from Shelburne Falls, Massachusetts. How random. We talk about familiar places: Newell Hardware, the Bridge of Flowers....

A friend of theirs took our picture. People love to have their picture taken with a hiker for some reason!

I sing in the visitors' center bathroom.

The acoustics are great!

You take my picture on top of the dam. I take a picture of you standing on your hands on the Smoky Mountain entrance sign.

You and I play the pole game, something we've done pretty much from the start of this walk. It kinda breaks things up and is fun.

Well, not so fun today 'cause it got a little rough. You wack me so hard in the shin with your pole that I grab my leg and fall to the ground sending out a string of expletives that would surely burn any good truckers' ear! So mad, am I at you, that, I stand right up and slam you as hard as I can with my pole.

Ashtray shouts, "Stop it, you guys! Just stop! You're gonna kill each other, this is plain stupid!"

I sit, crying, and watch, as my only- two –minutes- ago- smooth skin transforms itself into a bulging egg-like shape.

"Can you walk?" you quietly inquire.

"Uh, huh," is all that passes through the tears.

Pack still on, poles steadying my frame; I push myself up, take a deep breath and look at you.

"C'mon let's get going," you gently say and like ducklings, we fall in line.

So, now I mutter to myself, but just loud enough for you to hear, "I not only have a big bulging egg on my shin, but I have a sore rib from when you picked me up and spun me around the other day..... I mean really, I weigh 112 lbs.... and you weigh, whatever, you're a feakin' hulk, arm muscles the size of Gibraltar!"

...no   sympathy,   here,   from   you...   fending   for myself...whining, isn't working....so, I switch gears, smile and begin to laugh.... *What else is there?* You join in, too!

This is all I need: freedom, laughter and the woods.

At 2.7 miles we reach **Shuckstack Fire tower: 4020'**

I don't really want to go up, 'cause of that whole *I feel like I wanna jump thing.*

But, you say, "C'mon, you gotta do it"

"Okay, I'll try," and reluctantly, I slowly climb, and climb, and before I know it…

"Hey, I made it!" I exclaim. "Good job," you squeeze in, as I tentatively utter, "it's fine, *nice view … but,* I'm gettin' a little sweaty underneath, 'cause I wanna be down there on the ground and not up here, anymore… so…"

"Yah, whatever," you coolly reply.

Birch Spring Gap, 168.7 miles from Springer.

I am so tired. I cook dinner and give it to you and go to bed.

You hang the bags and set up for the night. We sleep on a rock platform.

Saturday April 27, 2002

Gourmet Dan is just up the hill from us. …very cool to reconnect…

You make up a rap and call it: "Pack it in! Pack it out!"

"Too bad you can't record that!" I say.

"I can," Dan excitedly says, as he begins searching, among his gazillion pounds of photography equipment, for a recording device. Once located and set up, you say, "So, now we have, for all future ears to hear: A Rap from the Smokies!"

A man on a horse rides in. Guess he's a riding ridge runner or something, but very cool nonetheless, to see a horse in the middle of nowhere.

I am so hungry. I eat three packages of Oatmeal, a little peanut butter, and an apple.

I hope I have enough food for this week!

It is quite windy and the threat of rain is eminent…to leave, or not, is a decision you are trying to make. Five miles to **Mollies Ridge 174.1 miles from Springer,** the next water and shelter, ten to

Spence Field, 179.7 miles from Springer, where you want to stay.
Doe Knob: 4520' 171 miles from Springer; Ekaneetlee Gap: 3842' 172.4 miles from Springer;
Arrive at **Mollies Ridge Shelter 3:30 A.M.** Rest

Then onto **Russell Field Shelter: 176.6 miles from Springer.** "…the largest grassy bald in the Smokies…" [Thru Hikers Companion, 2004 p. 29]

…dusk, just before Rocky Top. We wake people up. They already have the bear fence down and secured for the night. The ridge runner gets up. You go for water. Within seconds of you leaving, and while I sit next to the newly opened bear fencing, a bear wanders into camp.

"Oh, my god," I excitedly say, beneath my breath, while simultaneously thinking: *Where are you? You have to see this!*

This bear stands up on the picnic table. He reaches for the hung bear bags. Within several minutes our noise scares him off. You return with the water only to be met with my, "I SAW A BEAR!! My first bear on the trail!!

"Where," you ask.

"He was right here! Oh, my god! The thing was huge and he was standing on the table and he was trying to get the packs and then he ran off …that way…and…" as I point in the direction that we will be soon walking…

Now, prior to this point I am okay to hike wherever in the pack, but *now* I am definitely *not* being the caboose anymore!

The ridge runner says, "You are fools to hike at night. It is unsafe,"… blah, blah, blah… We pack up.

And, after coaxing a couple hiker friends, from the safety of their bear fenced shelter, to join our night hiking escapade up **Rocky Top: 5441' 180.7 miles from Springer,** we head out of camp.

It is the longest 4.9 miles ever…. in the mist and it is windy-as- all- get- out. I am thinking: *bear… I am hungry. Why didn't I eat more than those bars at the last shelter?*

...so steep, so foggy, so tired... Finally, when I think I can't give anymore to this mountain, someone from ahead yells, "C'mon, keep walkin', you're almost at the top!"

"Okay, sure, whatever...." In the darkness, I just methodically lift one foot, then the other...over and over again...until, I reach the summit.

I drop my pack on top of Rocky Top. It is so foggy I can't see anything. I can hardly see you. We sing the Rocky Top song, 'cause it's what you've been waitin' to do! *And* for miles and miles, I've been listening to you rehearse the stupid song and sayin,' "Can't wait to sing this on the mountain!"

"...Yah, good ole Rocky Top!" I echo.

Mission accomplished! I eat a bar, drink some water and confidently walk on into the night.

Thunderhead: 5527'181.3 miles from Springer; Mineral Gap: 5030' 182.3 miles from Springer; Brier Knob: 5215'

A rest or two along the way ... making coffee and just talking...

I am a fool.

...in this space of my own undoing

Finally, the pack comes off at **Derrick Knob Shelter: 186 miles from Springer,** the "former site of Crede Hall's herder cabin" [A.T. Thru Hikers Companion, p.29]

You set up the Taj Mahal and like sardines, the now, more than three of us, ready for sleep. Yah, we sleep within the recommended limits of the shelter!

Sunday April 28,2002 Upon waking... it is beautiful here. It is 11:30 A.M. Chores.

Blue sky, windy, sunny, and warm...

Inspiration: like a relentless knock on a barred door; keeps color at bay

I am not ready for the freedom to feel so thusly inspired.........

I don't want to play the *I can't keep up with you*, game, any more.

I don't want to rise to *any of the occasions* anymore.

My space is as moody as all-get -out!

Oh god. What a fool, I think, *I am lost, once again…off track.*

I must reroute myself from this mood. To self correct. Here goes…I'm trying.

Focus…*let the piano playing echo in my brain…. try singing…think about drawing… Okay, something is changing…* exiting. I end this entry with a toast to: inspiration and good health!

Driving into Spring will be the title of the mural and the writing.

a month in the woods… I am still learning.

I am so incredibly exhausted.

But not *so* tired, as to not stand in awe of a tree. …A huge shapely tree.

"Hey, let's hug this tree." you suggest. Now, I've seen you do this on occasion, but I never felt like I was a tree -hugging -kinda - person, *but* since you asked. I answer,

"Okay."

"What's the procedure here? Do we keep our packs on? Do we take 'em off? "I ask.

"C'mon, packs on or off, *who cares,* we're just hugging a tree here…" you say, making light of my logistical questions.

So, with chests pressed firmly against the knobby barked trunk the two of us stretch our arms out and around and with a little more effort are able to link fingertips and hug a tree! Yes, *that's right*! **We Hug A Tree!** Right *here* in the middle of nowhere. Hmm… mm… tree hugging could be my new favorite trail event. I am now on the lookout for BFT's!

And with that said and done, I continue, only to witness the beauty of a white carpeted hillside of Trillium. And, I mean a whole hillside! …and miniature iris at the stream crossing…

On eating: I can feel the food. The nutrients entering my energy depleted body.

I have two new blisters on my little toes and a little itchy stuff on my arm.

I don't know what I look like. I barely know how I feel. So…. this is a tentative state.

I am in gray zone.

Talking about the movie: "Out of Africa," you fall and cut yourself.

We rearrange a trail crossing sign for no other purpose than to have some fun out here… you, then, correct the arrangement…

Getting closer to Clingmans Dome… Ashtray is ahead, which isn't unusual except on this night, in our now weary state, you and I somehow find ourselves off the trail, and walking down what we too late realize is a drainage ditch, and not the A.T. at all! Great! All this down, is now an unplanned up. Crap! You turn around. I silently follow … up.

"Listen. Do you hear something?" You ask. "Hel… l… o… o ….Where are you guys…s..?" echoes through the still night air. To far away to realistically answer, and, hey, we got our own problems; like, we really don't know where the hell we are in this headlamp-lit -night! What seems like forever is probably only about a half hour before we reach the real A.T. and are once again three.

"Don't even ask," I say.

We climb up to the top of **Clingmans Dome Tower: 6643' 195.9 miles from Springer**

This is the highest point on the entire trail offering 360 degree views, which we will fully appreciate in the morning.

Group decision… We decide to sleep up here, although the sign clearly states: Camping Not Permitted. This sort of thing has never stopped us before, so up we go to get our yard sale on, unroll the bags and pads, and settle on the cement floor. The wind is howling. It is freezing cold. I have on everything that I own. Our bags are lined up against the outer wall. I fall in and out of a shivery sleep.

Monday April 29, 2002

Awake. *What's that sound?* I'm thinking, as my mind begins to unthaw. *It's a ... it's a lawn-mower! Holy crud, we're illegal up here!* and with that thought, I scramble, cram my stuff into the pack, and excitedly call out," C'mon….,c'mon…,Get up! c'mon, Get

Up! We're gonna be in trouble," …

Packs packed and on, in record time, we walk.

The lawn mowing person waves a friendly hello as we make our tower descent.

We pass a bussed -in school group on a field trip. I talk with a student about my walk and writing poetry.

"What the…" I say, as off to the right I notice a forest of dead standing trees. Forest rangers say that they are too expensive to clear so there they stand. The scoop on this is that, "The spruce forests of the Great Smokies are in a period of decline because of air pollutants and attack by the balsam wooly adelgid, a killer of mature fir trees." [Appalachian Trail Guide to North Carolina/Georgia: p.37]

We stand in the parking lot for a moment then, you stick your thumb out.

Hitch hiking into Gatlinburg, Tennessee. A guy named David stops.

"Where yah goin'?" he asks.

"Gatlinburg," you answer.

"Me, too," he says.

We hop in. *Well*, there is actually very little hopping *anywhere* with a forty pound pack!

There is a Dobro in the front seat.

"I'm gonna be performing at the gazebo in Pigeon Forge tonight," David begins and continues with, "You should come up and see me and next week I can take you White Water Rafting in Davenport."

Reflective randomness…

David: Roll my Bela Fleck… Drive… Blue Grass Sessions…..
…a ride to Gatlinburg, Tennessee; *is* it Tennessee? Following an
army truck off of Clingmans Dome

Modeski, Martin and Wood …7 miles from the highest point
on the trail this side of the Mississppi. I need triple A Batteries.
Spring iris in bloom, white somethings, Spring Beauties carpet the
roadside, dandelions, slept on top of Clingman's Dome lookout.
…Freezing. Roads carve out the hillside. Newfound Gap…,
Cherokee Chimneys…

9 miles. Pigeon Forge Park, Gatlinburg, Pigeon Forge Pass,
Dolly World on the right,

Micky D's on left, Ernest Tubbs recording studio, look for the
damn White Gazebo….

Gatlinburg, Tennessee. 195.9 miles from Springer

Ah! The beauty of the commercial mecca of Gatlinburg! After
a week in the woods this is a tad overwhelming!

We check into the Rainbow Hotel, shower and order a pizza.
Yah, we got our priorities down alright!

Food generates thought and I think*, what's the purpose of
tomorrow?* Which comes alongside a lyrical fragment… *why would
I try to put the colors of the day next to you?*

Tired…. rafting and mini golf, smiles and sunsets…..

an afternoon in Gatlinburg, Tennessee…

Tuesday April 30, 2002

I am so done with the trail hair maintenance thing. I make an
appointment to get my hair cut at Tony's Magic Touch.

You walk with me to the salon where upon I say, "just leave
me alone until the cutting and tinting is all done." You do not go far
enough away. I can see you and visually shoe you away with

several sweeping hand gestures. Guess you get my drift, because you leave.

Although a little anxious about the process, I settle, with a pre-sleep sort of comfort, into the well padded chair and tip my head back over the sink. She washes my hair and then begins to cut… No turning back now. Next, the tint and a little drying, before she asks, "Okay, what do you think?" "What's Tony think?" I ask. I'm thinking: *perky*! *This is so much fun. I want to do my nails!* "Thank-you! Thank-you! Thank-you!"

I pay and began to look for you. We go to the Hard Rock Café for a celebratory Margarita or two. Then it's back to the Rainbow Hotel…

So, when the day ends all I have is me inside this shell. What is this look about? Do you want to be?

a harbored pearl
turned waverider
on a clustered opalescent streetlamp- lit –lane
at this break of dawn

8:30 P.M. <u>Hair</u>: so visible, so transparent… what does it mean?

Oh, what do I do?

I speak. I feel. I walk.

May 1 Postcard Home:

Leaving now for 4 days- a raft ride in Davenport Gap on the Pigeon River. Then on to Hot Springs -saw a bear the other night. Clingmans Dome-the highest point on the trail-Talk soon, Love Mom.

My hair is definitely short. I am going to look in the mirror. My rib is sore.

The thought of hiking today in the rain is somewhat unappealing. I kinda want to check out more stuff here. There I go again, that whole tourist thing!

We have breakfast. Potatoes, eggs, bacon, juice, toast and lots of coffee...

"Guess we better think about headin' out soon," you say.

"Yah, the sun's coming out and now..." I answer.

"I want to shower first, though." I say. Although, there's little reward in being clean, when all I have to put on are my sweaty clothes....oh, well... with that said, I pack....

Ashtray is going to Florida to attend his uncle's wake. There is no surety that he will ever cross my path again.

I talk to his mother and tell her, that among other things, he is learning about the wildflowers along the trail. His parents tell him to keep hiking, so he stays.

Heading out of town: We go to the Whole Earth Grocery Store, Food City, and The Happy Hiker Outfitters to re- supply and mail stuff.

At the outfitters the owner takes our picture for the hiker photo wall.

My stuff consumes a corner of the shop. In true yard sale fashion! What a process... packing, unpacking, deciding what to send? What to keep? Where is it? And, do I have what I need for the next four days? How heavy is it all? Will I be able to carry my pack?

You wait patiently.

Well, this takes hours, but, *finally* I am set to go.

Then you say, "Let's have one last meal in town."

"Okay," I answer, no arm twisting here!

Remember: hikers are always hungry!

We go to the Burning Bush Restaurant. Pretty fancy for hikers... We settle in at the bar and you ask,

"Have you ever had a martini?"

I answer, "No."

You say, "Since this is a hike of firsts, how about your first martini?"

"Okay," I say.

Well, as my first Martini makes its way to the bar, I think…*hmm…mm… Cute little glass and it even has an olive, which I love, so how bad can it really be?*

But, one sip and the verdict is out: "Whew, this is nasty!"

"Give me a sip," you ask

"Help yourself, I gladly offer, "but I want it back."

"Why do you want it back if you think it's so *nasty?*" you ask me.

"'cause I want that marinated olive at the bottom of the glass," I reply as I proceed to down, what I fully suspect will be, not only my first, but my last martini, ever!

"Okay, that's done. I need a beer!"

The bar tender accommodates the request. I am pure entertainment for him at this point.

"Hey, can I order side dishes at this bar?" I ask.

"What would you like?" he asks.

"How about mashed potatoes and corn?" I say.

"No problem," he says, and within minutes, there, right in front of me is a heaping plate of buttered potatoes with sour cream and a side of corn. I am in heaven!!

He watches me like I'm about to set a world record or something, for eating the most potatoes in the least amount of time, and then with a smile on his face and probably thinking that there's no way, but I'm going to ask anyway, he poses the question, "Can I interest you in a dessert?"

"Well, ah sure…" I answer, mid gulp, and continue with, "Whaddaya got that's chocolate?"

"I've got just the thing for a chocolate lover. Let me surprise you," he replies.

Several minutes pass, before the bartender returns carrying an artfully constructed brownie sundae! He sets it in front of me and well….

Dessert done and still not quite ready to end this fun, you order another round for the road.

You pay and leave a generous tip.

Now, we are ready to hit the trail!

Ya, and I'm hitch- hiking again!

A couple going camping stops to pick us up. "You'll have to ride in the back." they say from the comfort of their warm, dry cab. They drop us at the trail head. It is late in the day, but that's what head lamps are for and we are night hikers!

The plan is that we will hike 10 miles today to Ice Water Spring Shelter, 13 to Tri Corner Knob Shelter, then 15 to make it to Davenport Gap Shelter for White Water Rafting with David-the Dobro playing, river guide who gave us a ride off Clingman's Dome.

May 1, 2002: Mt. Love: 6446' Mt. Collins: 6188', Mt. Collins Shelter: 5900' 199.8 miles from Springer; Newfound Gap: 5045' 203.8 miles from Springer. "U.S. 441/Newfound Gap: The only road crossing along the Trail in the Smokies." [A.T. trail Thru Hikers' Companion-2004.p.29]

It is dark, now. Headlamp on… It begins to rain… and we walk…I feel so tired.

You say, "You're doin' great, just a little further, we are very close to where we will set up the tarp." Believing that this down may in deed be the last of the night before rest, I become careless, loose my focus and before I know it I am lying face down on a mud and root tangled floor with a forty pound pack on my back! I lie there. Face, literally planted in the ground, mentally checking my vital signs: Where am I hurt? Am I hurt? Are my glasses broken?

"Are you okay?" you guardedly inquire.

I do not answer.

"Are you okay?" you pointedly ask, again.

I, again, do not answer.

Then you say, with an edge of irritation in your voice, "Jesus Christ, D, will ya answer me?"

I curtly reply, "Yes."

"Was that a *'yes,'* you're gonna answer me" or a *'yes'* that you're okay" you ask seeking clarification.

"Yes, to both," I softly reply as I try to get up.

This is a slower than usual process, given the nature of the ground and this over weight pack on my back. And, to further compound my aching, rain soaked, covered in mud state, I am unable to hold back a flood of tears.

You wait and watch patiently for me to get a grip before gently inquiring, "Are you ready to go on, now?"

"Well, yes. I guess," while thinking, *I'm a freakin' muddy mess. I'm wet to the bone. My knees are bruised and bloody and my rib is just plain aching with every breath.*

We continue, kinda -not, really, saying much of anything til the tarp site. We get in around 10:30 to the **Mt. Collins Shelter.** You set up the tarp. You hang the bags. I make mashed potatoes. You make jiffy pop! "Hey, where'd that come from?" I ask as you pass it my way. What a surprise! This is the comfort food that turns my evening around. Ah! to have popcorn in the woods chased with Fritos and half a Mounds bar. Life doesn't get much sweeter than this!!!

No doubt about it. No coaxin' me to sleep. I'm just glad to be in the bag! I'm spent!

…in the hills….in the rain, *yes,* it's raining, raining, like crazy. …a constant plinking on the tarp roof, water puddling outside my door.

I have one final, parting, pre sleep thought: *Help me remember the reason we choose not to stay in the shelter? Oh, yah, the whole bear enclosure thing….*

Thursday, May 2, 2002

James: works at the University *of* Bloomington, Ill. …a Caver. He says, "The deepest caves are in Mexico."

He takes a black and white photo of us and our yard sale and of you doing one of your signature hand stands.

"…love to see all them ruins," Ashtray says and adds,

"…they are the largest pyramid ruins in the western hemisphere."

"I go to the temple and pray on New Years," he tells us and continues with the

"The sun is on one side, and the moon is on the other side."

"I've never seen a volcano, but it's on my list," Ashtray randomly adds.

"Saw PoPo," James says.

Conversation sound bite: Oaxaxa covers 7-8000 miles…. Southern border…. stupid bowl hike…. 20-25 mile day hike… James.

Newfound Gap: 5045'

Parking lot mid day…. Lots of tour buses. I use the restroom. I get water from a drinking fountain. No pumping! It's quite hot and sunny.

Several of the well groomed travel writers from Canada walk my way and ask, "Do you mind if we take your picture and ask you a few questions for our magazine?"

"Okay," I say. They ask me about hiking the Appalachian Trail; give me a hug along with words of encouragement.

You give them a handstand.

The trek continues. Quite the long up from here… I pass a deer grazing. Still. …and unmoving from my way… I am in his place. …

There is a birds' nest in the side of the hill along the trail…little blue eggs and a noisy mother in a nearby tree.

…late day… **Ice Water Spring Shelter: 206.8 miles from Springer.**

We stop, eat peanut butter and bagels, carrots and chocolate and then decide to continue, even though the weather looks ominous.

Charlie's Bunyan: 5375' 207.7 miles from Springer, the Sawteeth, Bradley's View 209.6 miles from Springer.

About 45 minutes into the walk we stop to take a lot of photos from the rock- out cropping called: Charlie's Bunyan, which " got its name on a hike in 1929, when Charlie Conner and Horace Kephaty, an A.T. pioneer and famed conservationist of the period, discovered this spot, created by a landslide after a disastrous rain the same year. Upon reaching its summit, the two decided the rocky outcropping stuck out like a bunion on Charlie's foot." [Appalachian Trail Thru-Hikers Companion 2004:p.30.]

I am too scared to go out there with you. The 1000' shear drop might have influenced this decision some! I sit, wait, and watch as the gray-blue clouds move up and fill in the valley floor. "C'mon! We gotta get movin'" I call to you. "Okay" you quickly answer and are back in sight within minutes.

No sooner do we begin to walk, when the rain and lightening hits with all its glory.

"Holy…"

"Keep walkin'" The wind picks up with a force beyond belief. I have never experienced anything like this before. Too far away from safety, to turn back now, we continue on. Good decision or not, there is no time to ponder the point, for we are three hikers on the highest crest of the Smokies, in one of fiercest thunder and lightening storms of the season with full packs and ya, metal poles!

Is this a fitting place to die? …'cause that's what's about to happen to me…to us! Death on the A.T.! Natures' wrath is upon us. Trees crack, fall and split open all around us. You stop and say, "Put your arms around this tree." I do.

"Do you feel it moving?" you ask.

"Yes," I answer, as I feel the winds force vibrating through the tree, deep into my chest….

"Oh my *god*, this is *serious*!" I shout. "We could *die*!" "Should we ditch our poles?"

Adrenalin kicks in.

"No, just keep moving and be careful" you reply, with an uncanny sense of calmness given the situation.

How careful can one be given the circumstances? I think to myself

"Okay," I answer, as I watch trees bend further than they naturally should and think

This could be my last word, my last thought, my last visual…then…

A loud crack, lightening fells a tree just feet before my approach!

This can't be safe! My glasses are wet and foggy. Can't see…

Water sloshing around in my now, un-duct taped boots, I am completely soaked! The trail is a rushing stream bed littered with uprooted splintered trees! Whole sections of earth are relocated as this torrential burst leaves us now trail less. We bush whack.

I am completely exposed to the forces of nature. I look out across the churning cloud covered landscape. I'm at the same height as the lightening! It is hard to keep my balance as I venture across the rock carved knife edge. If ever I was close to death this is it! I stand at this point for only a moment.

I let the wind play with me as I pray, and I mean *pray*! I survive this!

"C'mon keep walkin," you pointedly call out.

I think *Nature is not to be messed with*…and continue to walk.

Peck's Corner Shelter, or a bit beyond, and now, **214.6 miles from Springer,**

Eight miles of night hiking and on the other side of the storm we stop. Exhausted… We set up camp and sleep.

May 3, 2002 This morning I have oatmeal and granola and am… drifting in an outta of sleep…

I sleep off and on 'til late afternoon. I am not so motivated today. Spent is a better way to describe me. All my gear is wet and I am drying out. I do not want to put on wet boots, but, I reluctantly do and start walking.

Guyot Spring [6200'], 221.2 miles from Springer; Mt Guyot [6621'] 221.3 miles from Springer."This section between Guyot and Cammerer is the section know as Hell Ridge named so because of the devastation caused by forest fires on the North Carolina side and because it was difficult to travel" [Appalachian Trail Thru Hikers Companion-2004. P.30]

Cosby Knob: 226.6 miles from Springer.

…and now, walking at night, telling the Out of Africa story again, in between sips of Wild Turkey. Ya, its doin' the trick!

We walk 15 miles **to Mt. Cammerer Side Trail: 5000' and Fire Tower: 5025' 229.9 miles from Springer.**
The fire tower is made of stone, offering a 360 degree view of the Smokies.

Mt Cammerer is a short distance off the AT, but you say, "It is worth the point whatever it is and it is the *middle of the night* and it is *raining* and it is an *enclosed shelter*!" *hmm... ...mm, I think. No hanging a bear bag, or setting up the tarp.* "Okay. I'm convinced," I answer and walk, the point whatever it is.… but, not any faster than my water- logged duck - taped boots can move me.

Ashtray gets there first and yells into the blackness, "Hey guys! You're almost here. Just a little bit further…"

Now, I see the headlamp light shining like a beacon in the night and pick up the pace a bit.

Altogether, inside, pack and boots off, stove out, sleeping bag ready and waiting.…I cook dinner inside the fire tower: Knorr Minestone Soup, Crazy Jane's salt, and a handful of noodles. I squeeze peanut butter right from the tube into my mouth. So satisfying! I break a blueberry bagel into the soup, Jarlesburg cheese [a personal trail favorite], a few chunks of a dried apple or two, water, and for dessert: the Almond Joy, I've had since

Gatlinburg! Doesn't get much sweeter than this!!

This is one side trail that has totally proven itself!

Its early morning, the kind of morning for me that falls not long after midnight, but that's me, a night hiker doing my thing…. catch the sunrise, and hope that the heat of the day will dry out my socks and boots… clothes are all damp and my food is running low.

Speaking of boots, mine are really trashed at this point. They are so covered with mud and have duct tape wrapped around and around and around and around the soles. So, *stylin*…

Saturday, May 4, 2002 A.M.

I wake up. I take a pee. I go back to sleep. I wake up for real at 10 and eat last night's dinner, nuts, and peanut butter. Wish I had some jiffy pop!

…beautiful view of the Smokies… I take a lot of pictures,

I hang out my socks to dry in the sun…make breakfast…

You comment: "We are all increasing our comfort zones." No comment.

I'm makin' pasta for breakfast and who knows what for dinner, 'cause that's about all I got left….

Then, as we are sitting on the fire tower steps, I hear voices. Several, soon to be picnicking, day hikers come into view. We talk as they unpack their lunches.

"Do you want any of our food? Because we brought way more than we can eat and we don't want to carry it out." the man asks.

Hmm… …mm… Let me think? …for a millisecond, because I do not want to seem overly anxious for their strawberry cream cheese bagels, then I politely ask, "Are you sure?"

They reply, "Yes, we're sure," as they proceed to give us their extra strawberry cream cheese bagels.

Trail magic happens at the most unexpected times! We eat, pack, and continue on.

The wind is whipping… "Can we, can you do another 15 miles today?"

"I'll try."

Tarp Talk…What's in a name? This is… me. It's me, my name spelled phonetically. If you think phonetically, this is how you pronounce it.

How many names can be spelled phonetically?

Bowler's Clan of the Highlander will be coming to get you. What is your nationality? Irish/Scotch…

You say my name wrong. I push your feet, which I know are already hurting and touching them, will irritate you. You say, "You're getting violent," and then, you deliberately say my name wrong again. I grab your foot with my hand. You retaliate. A minor scuffle ensues.

"C'mon, cut it out," you call out. I flip you the bird and stop.

Blue Sky…

You give me the weather report. The A.T. Trail report… Bowler…

"C'mon D, when ya gonna give up the extra weight you've been carryin' since Hiawassee?" you jokingly ask.

"Right now," I answer, as I take out a pack of Camels.

"*Jesus*, D, you really *did* have cigarettes!! You exclaim in shock and surprise and continue on with, "and ya don't even smoke!"

"Well, you know the whole back up thing," I calmly explain.

You never really quite believed I had them, but now deep in the Smokies, miles from any convenience store, there they are: my extra weight: a pack of Camels! …lifted…

The sky is changing. We are going to try and leave by noon. Yah, right!!!

Hand washing and bathing. I do my best, but… unlike having facilities readily available….. Monthly stuff……. you are sympathetic… softening rough edges…facial clues reveal….we are all human, so why would I expect more from you than I would from myself?

In keeping me positive and focused you randomly comment, "We are sleepin' in some of the best places."

"Ya, we don't ….. …around," you then add.

I think: *wish we had more popcorn for tonight*…oh, well…..

Davenport Gap Shelter: 1975' 234.2 miles from Springer:

"Named for William Davenport, who surveyed the state line through the park in 1821. The last, or first, GSMNP A.T. Shelter, was dubbed the "Smokies Sheraton" and had a facelift in 1998." [Appalachian Trail Thru-Hikers Companion: 2004. p.30].

Confidence and Fear: how interwoven.

Here I am so confident on where to place my feet, but so unsure of me. I am afraid.

Thinking and writing compounds emotions… Colorless and canvas less, I sit and I watch as tears fall, and subsequently stain this page, forever changing the hue of the paper.

Will this tear stained page fade and yellow over time? Who will wonder about such thoughts written on this day?

Don't ask me anything… 'cause I know nothing….. Nothing matters. …this existence…. this walk…… this filtering… is for more than a sip of water…stop…. too much to do, to think anymore…….alone

So, take me onward, up this mountain and down again.

pen in hand
melodic words   splashed on a page
reveal a cloistered thought

The depth of the forest is freeing.

I'm as I've never been. …fear and confidence… …who cares? Unconditional *what,* I can't even find myself for me anymore. Or can I? What is the answer to the question?

….the forest casting me a glimpse of free…Let me breathe…

Raw… remnants, subtle clues, currented this breath away

I pause to write. You are patient with, what turns out to be a rather long writing break. This pause will perhaps cost us a rafting trip. No pressure to move.

We are now in the Cherokee National Forest. We hike awhile, cross cascading streams and waterfalls surrounded by lush greenery. The Mountain Laurel is in bloom!

Saturday: May 4, 2002

It's early as we hike out of the Smoky Mountains. **Davenport Gap**: Eastern Boundary of the Great Smoky Mountain National Park.

We are too late to meet David.

Crossing the **Pigeon River 1400', 236.7 miles from Springer,** we sit in the middle of the bridge and have a snack before heading across the highway and back into the woods. It is ever so lightly raining.

Only a short walk brings us to **Standing Bear Hostel**. A cluster of fine crafted shelters. One has a handmade quilt on the bed and a stream running beneath it. There is an outhouse/shower, and a gathering spot with a fire pit.

This place has such a great feel about it. The water, the shelter, the people! *Or*, is it that I've been in the woods so long that I'm more appreciative of humankind and goodwill.

We decide to stay. I do the laundry for us, as well as Curtis's family. You make a beer run.

For now, the beer and my feet are companions in the cool water. My feet are still pretty trashed.

…Sitting outside by the stream with several other hikers.

I cook a little dinner, using the last of the food bag stuff which is quite unappetizing and just doesn't cut it. So, I leave it. I don't clean my pot. Try something different tomorrow after shopping. Can't wait to get to the store and get some Fritos, pretzels, bananas, and jiffy pop. Except for the bananas, its salty junk food I crave!

I do love hiking. Why? What else might I do? Not for me to say.

You come inside the cabin and ask, "Have you completed your thinking and writing yet?"

And I answer, "Almost."

Then, you say, "You're not ready to go home yet."

I look up, somewhat perplexed by the statement and ask, "What do you mean?"

….no comments from you, end of conversation….back to writing…

I must sleep now. My feet must heal.

In the night I awake and think…..*to continue…. to continue on, with what I have come out here, to do or find out*….rationalize, …the cornerstone of hiking is fun, talking, and listening. ….the group I'm with is good.

So what's to think about? ….to sleep in the morning, to snore in the night, *I don't snore or do I? How would I know?* And to walk through the forest …It is all so freeing.

Who am I really? …unfolding, effortless… I… more… or less… more… now, than before… peel away the layers of fear that falsely shape a lifetime… I long for who I am. Sleep.

Standing Bear Hostel: Sunday, May 5, 2002

So, I'll while away these ponderings….
               of gauze like mists
          held snug in a coastal embrace

Absence of fear is but an open heart left to dream. …keep writing.

You say, "It is better that you write and not think about a lighter."

"What?"

No response.

Guess I must have lost the lighter or something, anyway….

So, when I write I continue to dream and when I dream I am free. Once again, words flow with ease from my pen across this page. …the soft feel of the paper beneath these page holding fingertips…. Some combinations are just, some are not. So, I am mincing not these words, in order to find peace. Peace in this heart, peace in this mind, peace will be as I find it or it finds me. ...inside or outside myself...

Mistakes are not mistakes. This world no longer exists for me. I am ridding my mind of useless debris, slowly and surely, unlearning all the characteristically patented disciplines of the past. The ones handed down generation to generation. A false sense of teaching, just because one generation said it must be so, must another suffer? I think not. I will continue to search within myself for the answer.

To break this cycle of false guidance,

To open the door and begin anew,

Love is the base.

Control of others is fear based. If one thinks by teaching via the control method, then love will not flourish, love will die, the soul within will perish and all will be in a state of unrest. Control, fear, confidence, love, lost... Am I getting closer to the essence of being?

Don't know. Rest, and then get on with the process. I am alone.

I am still conflicted as to continue or not. Will get back to that thought, later, as right now this zero day is just too sunny and comfortable for any serious thinking.

I did sleep well, though and am about to take a *long* shower and then just sit around.

Granola and pizza for breakfast!

Hey! Today is Cinqo de Mayo or however you spell it! And I am going to celebrate it in style!

You say, "Have a beer?"... "Sure, why not!" I reply, as I take a seat by the fire pit.

The ensuing alcohol enhanced conversation begins with: "Where are you from?" ...

"Hey, what's your name again?"... "We're hiking the Sea-to-Sea Trail"....

"What's that?"..."Your name again is..?"

"Where ya' from?" ... "Hey, Curtis, you got any art materials kickin' around?"

"Yah, I think the kids have some stuff. Let me go into the house and check."

Two beers in me, and with the newly found art supplies, I begin to paint. I do a couple of drawings of the cabin, one just to get to the purple.

Then I excitedly say, "Let's do a drawing together!"

You turn my way, with a, *what are you talkin' about ... and how's this gonna work look,* as I animatedly continue with, "I'll start, and work for a few minutes, then I'll pass the paper to you, and you just add your interpretation of the landscape, before handing it to the next person. Okay?"

"Okay." and I begin to paint...

I leave them both there.

"I'll frame these. It's another project, but I like projects!" Curtis says with a smile.

Cowboy coffee cooking, guitar playin' and the thought of goin' bowling at 5:30... I still owe you some stupid amount of games and a few cocktails!

Curtis calls his wife at the restaurant [Did I mention she owns a Mexican restaurant?] and she's all for family bowling!

My feet are so swollen. Can't fathom the thought of squeezing these blistered moleskin- patched feet into form fitting bowling shoes!

Oh, well, for now I'll prop them up and rest some. And, with this rest comes the thought that later tonight we will be walking once again....

Afternoon

So, *where's* the little package I had this morning? It has the magnets, the clippers, my barrettes, my foot repair stuff, and tape in it. What am I to do? Hopefully it'll turn up, and if not... Well, it's gone. I did just use stuff from it this morning, in the shower, and now… here I am stressing, again… sitting here thinking: where *is* this stuff? I begin dumping the contents of all my stuff sacks out on the bed… the table…on the floor….all the while thinking…did someone take it? What a thought! Who would want that stuff, anyway? How do I get rid of this stressor? It's just dumb stuff.

Looking still… packing, unpacking I have so few things … where is it? …calm down, it'll turn up…I hate it when things are missing.

We are on our way to bowl at Victory Lanes in Newport, Tennessee with Curtis's family. I owe you seventeen games! So, you will be definitely cashin' in. We bowl thirty games at $2.25 for a grand total of $67.50, plus shoes. Three hours of bowling and beer. And not just any bowling, it is *extreme* bowling!

"What is that?" you might ask

"Well," I might answer, "*extreme* bowling is bowling two lanes at once, so you are always bowling."

There is no sitting when bowling with the bowler!

Scores go like this 168,148,152 and you finally break 100! For the later half of the night it is disco bowling. Crazy fun! Good lanes, good balls!

I want to buy the green number eight ball!

We get back to the Hostel around ten and pick up packing where we had left off.

We have a few beers, [as if that would help get us going any quicker!]. I eat the Fritos, two bananas and the rest of the pretzels.

You guys begin singing, *"Wool socks they never get dirty, the longer you wear them the stronger they get, Wool Socks…"*

You play the chords on your Takamine trail guitar. I surprise myself, and actually hear my voice rhyme and sing right along with you.

This is one of the hardest places to leave. The music is flowing.

We are not in any hurry, and yet, we are preparing to go.

Curtis comes up to the cabin with coffee for all of us and says, "Why don't you stay another night? Night time's no time to go inta the woods."

"Well," we explain, "we are night hikers and it's time to get walkin,' "

May 6, 2002

We hang out until about 12:30 A. M.

You strap on your pack, then me, mine.

Watching us, Curtis sadly says, "You *are* fixin' to leave, *aren't you*? Don't leave me," he adds.

So, with headlamp poised, duct -tape-secured –boots on, pack on, and poles in hand. We head out.

I walk slowly. So...o...o...o slowly. I try to find my stride, lifting first one foot then the other, counting each step in an effort to distract myself. I am plain exhausted and falling behind...as we wend our way up Snowbird, Mt...

You come back down the trail towards me and say, "Here D, drink this, it'll get you up the hill."

"What is it?" I ask.

"Never mind, just drink it," you hastily say, while handing me a can of something, which even under my headlamp has an indistinguishable label.

"Okay," I reluctantly answer and begin to drink. Well, I've almost downed the entire can when I hear you matter- of- factly state, "Red Bull."

"What!!" I instantly blurt out and continue to be verbally all over you with, "Oh! My God!! You mean I just drank bulls whatever!!"

"*Jesus*, calm down... will yah ...anyway..."

"Uh, huh, yah, sure," I laughingly reply, before resuming a slightly more energetic gait thanks to Red Bull!

Yea! I made it up the steep part of Snowbird. ...Nobody but me cheering, as I near the top... I stop... look around at the dark woods, and rest.

I am alone….which is not to unusual and I am not to worried 'cause I know I'll catch up….you are probably a mile ahead or something…....

I tell myself: pay attention….*watch for the white blazes, so you don't get lost…*

Great! I have to pee. What should I do? If I take my pack off, how will I put it back on?   … Oh, I really have to pee, can't ponder the what- if's too long… make a move here, so, psyching myself up, I whisper to myself, "This is it"… "I know it can be done 'cause other girls have told me they did it"…."I've heard their strategies for performing this seemingly freeing and monumental feat"… So nows the time, I *am* going to do it…

"I am going to pee standing up!"

Decision one made. Now for decision number two: Finding a good tree. This shouldn't be too hard, 'cause after all, I'm in a freakin' forest! Ah, here it is: *the perfect tree!*

I shut off my headlamp and pee for the first time, with my pack on, standing up!!

"Hmm… …mm… not bad…easier than I thought…how convenient…, " I'm sayin' to myself, while, at the same time feelin' pretty dam proud of the accomplishment.

Okay, with that little bit of business taken care of, I continue on the trail.

I can't wait to tell you. I walk and I walk and I walk some more…. kinda caught up in reminiscing the whole peeing -standing -up- thing, well perhaps a little too caught up in it 'cause from somewhere on the barren top of Snowbird I hear your voice calling.

"Dee…e…e…, Dee… e…e…e!"

"What?" I answer.

"D, *where* are you?" you yell out.

"I don't know! Where are *you*?" I reply as I spot your beacon and you mine.

Quite pointedly you yell out, "Jesus bowler *answer me when I call!!* Where the hell have you been?"

"I didn't see the turn, I reply and continue with …and, and…" feeling that my personal accomplishment has now lost its charm, I blurt out anyway…. "… and I peed standing up!"

You do not seem particularly impressed.

Still, I'm mildly annoyed that my peeing is not greeted with more exuberance, as I quietly follow you across the barren mountain.

Finally, together after a long uphill five mile climb up **Snowbird Mountain: 4263',** we huddle up against the air traffic control satellite building.

I have an apple and we hang out for awhile.

The city lights below, a 360 degree view of the night…

The stars are amazingly bright. "What's that constellation?" "Do you know that for sure or are you just makin' it up?" "Okay, I get it."… *"That's why they named it that!"*

We continue on until 4:30 A.M. and find a nice camp site.

You start a fire and we stay awake 'til the sun rises. "What are the colors?" you ask.

"I see rose madder, light blue, robins' egg blue and orangey striped pink," I recite dreamily, as if my fingers are actually moving them on paper.

Sunrise. 6:37 A.M.

I go to sleep.

You try, but, then decide to chance it and not hang at bear bag- as it is daylight and we have a fire. Ah. The power of justifying a moment!

See flowers I, need to, or rather wish to, identify.

Mountain Laurel and Poison Ivy everywhere…

I open my eyes at 8:30 and psyche myself up to crawl outta this warm bag to take a cold- air- pee …I pee in the path which is *so* taboo but, I can't risk getting poison ivy on my butt… … with that done I return to the warmth of my bag.

I sleep til 11:45 where upon I get up to pee, again and then stay up for real because,… well, by now I am hungry ….so I fix some granola with water and a little powdered milk and chase it with a mini lemon pie.

I do a pen and ink sketch of you sleeping and write in my journal.

My vitamins… Where are they? I have a stuffy nose and throat is a little scratchy.

It is a beautiful, warm sunny day. …cirrus clouds…

I think I'll take a nap now and start walking whenever.

Are we trying for 15 miles today?

Thinking about going home… But… how will I blend, back, into a life left behind?

I watch you, there, sleeping, head elevated, shirt off, in this forest.

The portrayal of this path -walking, night -hiking trio is as complete as it can be.

My muscles toned, my mind no longer fitful … able to let life in unencumbered.

To laugh with you, too is…is, what it is, so…next, for me is: singing out loud!

From the ridgeline and this unofficial campsite, not too far beyond Snowbird Mountain, I pack up and begin my walking day or afternoon, as it is now.

Ground Hog Creek Shelter: 2900', 244.7 miles from Springer; another Deep Gap, then Brown Gap: 3500' 247.6 miles from Springer; and across Max Patch Road, N.C. 1182 , 4250' 250.3 miles from Springer.

I walk alone, which really isn't even worth mentioning, as I walk alone a lot…

Crossing the road, then a stream, and through endless rhododendrons, I reach the fence and steps at the lower edge of Max Patch. I drop my pack, sit, and wait for you.

I eat a bar and take out this journal. Seems I do a lot of waiting….

Anyway, in the midst of this wait time, a rustle in the grass catches my attention…. and, to my surprise, out pops a bunny! Oh, my god! …a wild rabbit! I internally exclaim, as my hands rise into the air and then settle gently against my cheeks.

Where are my people? I ask myself and continue with…*get some control; it's only a freakin' rabbit!* … not so unusual given where I am, but…

I continue my observation of this little wild animal until he disappears into the tall grass… what fun, I think and begin to pack up.

I enter the field. I hear voices, your voices. I pause and hope. Sure enough, it is you and with this confirmed I ask, "What took you so long?"

You answer, "*Well*, we met someone on the road, who took us to the store, and hey, we got you some Apple Cinnamon Oatmeal."

Well, that just fixes everything, 'cause I love oatmeal! All is good.

Then, in true 'D' animated form I tell the bunny story before we begin to climb the steps that will bring us to **Max Patch Mountain: 4269'.** "The site of an old farmstead and logging camp, Max Patch was originally forested, but early inhabitants cleared the mountain top to graze sheep and cattle. In 1982, the USFS purchased the 392 acre grassy top mountain for the A.T. and now uses mowing and controlled burns to maintain its bald appearance." [Appalachian Trail Thru -hikers' Companion: 2004.p.32.]

Max Patch is everything and better than I had been told. It is an amazingly huge wide open, high altitude grassy field.

Several people are flying a kite and there is one tent set up.

"Hey, I recognize that tent!" and in the same breath, excitedly yell out, "It's Gourmet!"

Hugging now, and happy to be reunited, you ask, "Hey, you wanna take that thing down and night hike with us?"

"Sure, okay," he casually replies and begins to take down his tent.

Sitting quietly we watch the sun sink low before heading on over the mountain, to the back side of Max Patch, where we stop.

A little stone wall accepts my back.

You make coffee.

Gourmet gets out some airplane samples.

I bring out my carefully packed fritos. This oughta get us through the night!

Packs and headlamps on, we continue our trek.

Now, walking at night can be a challenge, especially after a little trail pick- me- up.

We rhythmically move along to our own thoughts, just thinking…spread out…maybe over a mile….then…

"Hey, you guys, do you hear something?" I call out.

The forest is as silent as ever as you strain to hear *something.*

"Nope," you answer from up the trail.

"No *really*. I can hear a voice," I shout back to you, and ask,

"Who's ahead of you? Let's do a name check."

So, you call out each trail name to determine if we are all here.

All of us answer loudly, then, I hear this faint and distant response. "*That's* the voice I was hearing!" I excitedly yell out.

"Where are you?" I worriedly, call out into the pitch black night.

"Don't know," comes back through the darkness, but, stay put and I'll find ya."

Still, hundreds of feet apart, this string of nighttime walkers sit and wait.

Finally, I see a lamp! It is Ashtray. All is well. We walk, bunching up, now, to hear his story.

"I somehow got off the trail and was on the other side of the stream bed in a field, before I figured somethin' wasn't right….and…."

As good as any place to set up camp.

May 7, 2002 Lemon Gap, NC.1182 Tennessee: 107 3550' 256.5 miles from Springer; Walnut Mountain Shelter, 257.8 miles from Springer.

In the morning Gourmet cooks pancakes with real maple syrup for breakfast. Gourmet is not called Gourmet for nothing, and now I know why!

You bravely help me tape my nasty blistered feet.

I re-Duct Tape my boots, put on the pack and say, "I'm ready."

"Well go on, we'll catch up to you," you encouragingly say.

I walk along and not too far from the shelter I approach a footbridge, which is really no big deal, *but* at this particular bridge there is a rather large, long, black snake!

I stop, step back, and excitedly call out, "Guys"... "Hey!!"...

You respond with, "What is it, D?"

"There's a snake here!" I yell back.

"Just go around it," you instruct.

Well, there is no way that I am taking one more step in any direction that brings me closer to that snake as I turn and hurriedly retrace my steps back to the shelter.

"Whaddaya doin' back here?" You ask.

"You gotta see this snake! It's huge!" I excitedly say, in my now adrenaline heightened state then, breathlessly add, "*And*, I'm not going near that footbridge until one of you checks this out."

You get up and reluctantly walk down the trail with me whereupon I point out the snake which miraculously is still sunning it self. One strategically planted pole near the snakes' head both startles and sends it into the wooded hillside.

I hate snakes!!

Bluff Mountain: 4686', 260.2 miles from Springer; Big Rock Spring, 261.8 miles from Springer; Garenflo Gap: 2500', 264.3 miles from Springer; Deer Park Mountain Shelter 267.7 miles from Springer.

….all part of the15 mile trek to a destination

It is hot today. My feet are killin me. I walk alone.

…heading into… **Hot Springs N. C., 1326' 270.9 miles from Springer**.

...showy orchids, lily of the valley, yellow lady slipper, orange azalea, mountain laurel…

This is one of the prettiest and longest downs ever! I can see the little town below and I want to be there. …such a tease!

Dusk settles in around me and I find I am alone, although I am so close to town, I'm not too concerned.

Coming out of the woods, I pass a hostel and a building which is the work center for the French Broad Ranger District.

"…Which way to town?" I ask, as I have no idea which way to go, and because I don't carry a data book.

"Take a left and head right on down Bridge Street. That'll take ya where ya wanna go," he tells me.

Hard top under my feet… I walk. There it is….

Hot Springs!

I locate the pub, enter, see you and proceed to dump my pack in an adjoining coat room. I find a place at the bar and order a beer and a pizza. Done for the day…

Conversation follows that first satisfyingly long sip. "Where are we staying?" I ask you.

"Haven't a clue," you answer.

The bartender, recognizing our dilemma, hooks us up, when he says, "You can sleep in a field near town for free. The only hitch *is*… that you *have* to be out early."

"No problem," we answer. Although, in reality this may pose a problem, for we are not known for leaving any place early!

We finish our food and have a few more beers. Come closing time the bartender drives us out to the field. No tarp tonight, no bear bag; just us, rowed up on the ground.

Wednesday Morning May 8, 2002

Come morning I am damp with dew. Still tired… gotta move… 7:30 … sound of nearby traffic… pack up my stuff … wearily put on the pack and head out for breakfast.

Next order of business: get a hotel room!

That done, you say, "I'm going to Ashville to visit a friend."

"I'm taking a shower, unpacking, and going nowhere," I say. "See yah."

Between the time I take off my boots and finish my shower, I notice just how swollen my feet are and that my ankles are rash-red.

This looks pretty bad so, I decide to go to the local clinic. They can't see me today, so I make an appointment for Thursday.

I am losing my voice, allergies I guess. I'm self diagnosing that the foot thing may just be poison oak.

5/8/02 Wednesday Mid morning: Shopping at the outfitters with Ashtray; ….new hiking shoes, Tevas, a new cook pot, which my stove fits into! a black Kavu hat, food, thin socks: immediately named my bowling Bridgedales! 'cause they are both, stylin'hiking socks and just the ticket for those form fitting bowling shoes! Ashtray waits and watches, for what must have seemed like forever, for me to decide which size shoes fit best.

"Whaddaya think? I know my feet are swollen now, but my real size is 9 ½ and they only have these in 10's, they have to be right, I'm going to be living in these shoes for… …what if they don't work out… then, I'm stuck…" I ramble on to him, but mostly am weighing the pros and cons of this with myself.

Okay, this is ridiculous! Just pick one and get on with it! I tell myself.

Montrail size 10.

Postcards Home

Hi, I'm in Hot Springs. Saw a bear. A large snake, rabbits; and the mountains are amazing. Going to sit in the Hot Springs today. Shower @ the campground. Boots are destroyed so I'm getting sneakers and gaiters-otherwise OK. Next day we leave. 6 days out. Talk to you soon. Love D.

Hi, mailing these on the same day 'cause I'm at the P.O. I do miss everyone. This experience is unbelievable. The people I'm meeting are amazing. From Hot Springs we are hiking to Erwin, Tn. Probably 6 days out. Its 80 degrees sunny and good to be in town. Beer never tasted so good! I've lost weight- now at 110 lbs. probably. Tan. Sore muscles and have poison something on my legs. Spirits good though. Have great hiking buddies. Love ya, D.

Afternoon: Ashtray arranges a White Water Rafting trip down the French Broad River.

"No, I don't want to do this… too dangerous…." I begin, before being cut off with,

"C'mon, you have to, D"…

Talked me right into it!

I hop in the van and off we go. At the rivers edge I get a few basic instructions on how to stay in the raft, but I really have no clue. Life vest and helmet on… I am really scared, but…hey, once this thing gets going, there's no time to think, and furthermore, what's *not* to love about the adrenalin rush of Class 1, 2, & 3 rapids!!

Three hours later and I'm *still alive*, but done for now, with this experience!

I agree to drive the van, while you continue to raft on down the river to Hot Springs.

…Stackhouse Road, Barnard and Walnut. … No license, no glasses, no clue. This is a trip!

Ashtray is already back when I pull in.

I walk to the motel, shower and then return to the pub for dinner: spaghetti and marinara sauce and salad with raspberry vinaigrette and a good glass of merlot.

Thursday A.M. May 9, 2002

I go to the doctors today for my swollen feet.

My voice is barely recognizable and the rash on my ankles has now spread further up my legs. The nurse takes a chest x-ray for the cough and sore rib.

Then, as part of the routine exam, she discovers a fibrous mass in my left breast. "May I suggest you have a mammogram, dear" she almost in a whisper advises, as my emotional flood gates simultaneously release more than a bucket of tears, "and may I set one up for you at the hospital in Ashville?"

"Um..Well…No, I gotta think about what all this means. I'm in the middle of a hike. I hadn't anticipated that this visit would be any more than you tellin me why my feet are swollen and…. why I have a rash on my legs and…. why I'm losing my voice….and giving me something to fix all these things," I answer, not really responding to her original question.

"Okay," she said and softly continues with, "may I suggest that you at least have one when you get home?"

"Sure," I said while thinking to myself, *that she may suggest anything she wants, but….*

Alone. I cry as I get dressed. I cry as I leave the office. I cry as I walk down the street to the motel. I cry as I look at you.

"What's the matter?" you ask. I chokingly begin. You take in the information.

Sobbing, I manage to continue, "…and, I have to pretty much stay in bed for a few days, keep my feet elevated… and think about this whole mammogram thing!!"

You, not missing - a - heart - beat - respond, "Hey, you do, what ya gotta do.

"We'll wait for you, while you rest and figure stuff out," is met with both an indescribable sense of comfort and relief.

I am a train wreck.

The new plan: You guys will slack pack some miles and I will rest.

So now, comfy on the bed, foot elevated, I watch T.V. the kinda thing I might dream of when I'm hiking in three- day- old crusty socks held in by duck- taped boots and sleeping under a rain-puddled tarp, but in reality this is kinda boring, …until you pop in and suggest, "Let's go down to the bridge."

Thursday afternoon "Okay. I guess I can walk a little, although my feet are at least twice their size and I can't bend my toes, and I can't even see the bones in my ankles, but, sure, I'm game!" I answer.

"Where's this bridge, anyway? I ask as I grab the camera, a Nalgene of water, and hobble out the door….but not really caring, 'cause I could sure use a walk!

Along the way you stop and buy some beer.

The railroad tracks head north outta Hot Springs to the bridge. The famed bridge: The jumping bridge.

"I tested it out while you were at the doctors," you matter - of - factly tell me.

Upon arrival, I watch as you walk out to the middle of the bridge, climb over the spotted green and rust steel side and, way too casually in my opinion, jump off…. into the French Broad River. Fact: The water beneath the bridge is 70 feet deep, which does little for me in the way of alleviating safety concerns.

"C'mon D. you gotta try this!" You breathlessly call out upon surfacing.

"Are you crazy? I'd kill myself doin' that," I call back, from the safety of the gravel bank.

You walk up and take several more jumps, while I safely continue to take pictures, *instead* of risking my life.

I want to get a better shot, so I walk out onto the bridge.

And thinking all the while…*it's a long way down... can't go there... ...like to, but...*

I position myself to capture the moment [a series of shots of you on the bridge, in the air, entering the water,] when I hear…Oh, my god! What's that sound?

"It's the freakin' train whistle!" The whistle sounds once again, and then this massive rolling structure rounds the bend…

"Holy Shit, the train is coming!!"…. **"..Jump!!"** ….

No time to think. What to do? Jumping is not an option.

The stage is set: you are high above on the iron structure, several others are on the bridge extensions beneath the track bed, and, well, I am, still midway on the track.

All players jump and meet the rivers surface within moments of the bellowing trains' crossing.

I run ahead of the train, no, I *fly ahead* to the safety of the crushed gravel area abutting the bridge. . to be within milliseconds, dwarfed by this iron behemoth,… heart racing …vibrations resounding through my body… sparks flying off the iron …and think

If I reach out I will be able to touch…Hey, those wheels are big! How long is this train? Thank God I wasn't any further out on the bridge….what if I had been further out on the bridge and had to jump?... where are you? Did the jumpers survive? C'mon, train, get on with it and end!

Finally, the caboose…I wave, the customary wave. He returns a wave and a look of surprise…

Now, to locate people… Dan, who has my camera, is still coiled on the steel support beams beneath the track bed.

"You mean you were under the train?" I ask

Those who bravely jumped were walking up the path, laughing and, visibly ready for a drink.

Scant little time is given to reliving the moments past and what ifs, before you get back to the order of the day: Bridge Jumping *Take Two*!!

You climb the fifty feet and gracefully cast yourself out into the air, your arms out wide for a moment, then hugging your shins, letting out a primal sound before you connect and disappear beneath the waters surface.

You climb the bridge two or three more times performing summersaults, flips, swan, and jack- knifes with such ease. Just so amazingly beautiful!

You, floating in the air, falling free into the French Broad …adrenalin high…is all I can imagine. You push risk beyond the envelope, right to the max….

I walk back to Hot Springs, go to the bank, the Pub, the outfitters, pack my bag and write a little before I take a nap.

Postcard Home:

to be continued. Spent the day going to have my feet checked. Eating. And talking with fellow hikers. Probably be home end of May. Leaving here Mon. A.M. walk for 11 miles then camp is the plan. I've gone 268 miles I think, so far. Spirits are good and I'm loving every minute of walking by myself in the woods. Take care. I love you. MOM

cont. Postcard Home

Say hi to everyone. Still in Hot Springs. There is a festival here this weekend and my feet are needing a rest. Great talking with you all. Am sending a package for you to open. The green bag has all the treats for all. Thanks for all the support! I'm working at a Pub to help pay for the room or maybe to pay for the food-went bowling last week with a bunch of hikers. Will try out the springs soon. Talk to you later, Love, MOM

Thursday night Dinner out consists of mashed potatoes, corn and a veggie burger!

"Hey, Joe can I borrow your van to go bowling?" You ask.

He says, "Yes!"

So, you put out the word and in no time we have a group to go bowling. You get the van and drive the Florida Trio to Max Patch then come back for us.

I say, "I think the lanes close at nine."

You call the bowling alley.

"They are open 'til ten. So, load in," you say and we're off to Newport, Tennessee!

On the way we stop to pick up a few of the necessary pre-bowling cocktail ingredients.

Victory Lanes… The owner gives us the shoes, "No Charge." We ask and bowl three lanes at a time: extreme bowling.

The manager/owner gives us all little wooden bowling pins…we pose for a group shot …

What a great night!

white noise:
a cacophony of clashing
wordlessness lacking vocalization

Drop the van off.

Go to the rental house. Two hikers have bikes! I borrow, what I all too soon discover is, a brakeless bike and ride the mile down hill into town. It's 1 A.M. and I'm riding a bike with you through the empty streets of Hot Springs.

…so surreal… I'm just kinda crazy free tonight.

Early Friday morning about 1:30 AM Back at the hotel for a few drinks… ….people gather in our room…

"I am a fire juggler," Joe says, somewhere in the flurry of predawn conversations.

"Hmm…mm… sounds entertaining," I hear.

"I'll be back in a few, just gotta run and grab my sticks," he tells us.

"You got any fuel? Ashtray asks. "Ya, I think so…I answer as I head towards my pack.

You take photos and Joe juggles fuel laden fire sticks.

Yah, right here in the wee hours of the morning, outside the hotel room in downtown Hot Springs!

It is awesome.

I am so tired.

"Hey, let's go the springs."

It's 3 A.M. on Friday morning. I want to go, but I wouldn't be writing this if I did, plus my foot has had enough for the day. It is still swollen to about twice its normal size and tight. I will go to sleep now or so I thought but you turn on the TV and we watch a movie about a hairdresser from Scotland who goes to L.A. and wins platinum scissors.

Friday May 10, 2002

You wake up at 6:58, not moving too fast. Me, I'm up and in the shower, 'cause I need to…. What's *need to*, mean anyway?

I go to the diner for breakfast.

Call home. Still thinking about the mammogram…. We'll see about that…

Friday May, 10 4:14 P.M.

Here's what consumed my day: Had lunch and bought t-shirts for the Jacob and Lucas, 2 key chains: one for Emily, one for Jacob, and stickers for the car. …mailed my fleece vest and the little bowling pins home… …sent two post cards… …vacuumed the room. …*bee..cause* my other reality is that, the hotel room at this point is sleeping six! I clean the room during the day to help my smoking credit card *and* to more importantly spare the cleaning service the chaos of our lifestyle.

Yes, I've been given permission to access the hotel cleaning supply room. I don't own the hotel, but…I'm in with the management… and now with that done, I am finally putting my feet up, amazing how…doing so little can take the better part of a day!

Never did get to the spa, oh well…

You slack pack fifteen miles today.

You try to decide on dinner. I try to write. Tangents…

The music fest is this weekend. Ashtray will work 'railroad track security,' whatever that means. So, maybe we'll meet him on the tracks with our beer and snacks.

You still haven't slept …think it's been 2 days… awesome! Coffee and sheer will.

"Too busy to waste time sleeping," you say.

room conversation:

"…feelings… you're from Va.? …you're from Tenn.? …you're from Mass.? What happened last night? …Oh man, I left my pack at the Outfitters…. I even forgot my pack was at the Outfitters…Sittin' pretty…. Dumb -ass hiking spice, Cadet, Home Boy, Trail Angel, trail magic. Enjoy Hot Springs. …Mother of Cardboard. D.J. parties are the funniest parties in Steamboat Springs. …On the cliffy side of the tracks. See the view from the outfitters; see some girls in summer dresses."

Friday night

We sneak into the festival. I feel sick to my stomach.

Dwarfed by towering oaks, fairy lights illuminate flowing skirts and tanned skin as I step sideways. A little movement, that's all it takes, plus a little dancing…Totally revived.

Toots and the Maytals, D.J. Logic: check out these groups.

Saturday, May 11, 2002

"I am the master of my own destiny, no one is pullin' me on a string," Jester.

"I love free," you say.

We all sit in this hotel room and listen as Ashtray talks about staying and living here. How could this be? Saturday night Ashtray gives away all his stuff. Moving: Here's what I think about that.

on the very second

its chrome hand swept one

a string of words,

"I don't long for anything. I am."

hit the floor like a ball of chaos

and the once arrested pulse

beneath a daisy -blue, button - down dress

took flight

Postcard Home *I am at the Smokey Mountain Diner. It is packed so I don't anticipate eating for an hour. Maybe I should volunteer to help! Oh, well, I have a cup of coffee and a large O.J. went to the River Festival last night. Heard the band Hobex. Check it out. They have MP3's on the internet or however you access the MP3's HOBEX.com I talked with the drummer and he said the band is getting signed next week and he gave me a CD which I'm mailing home. ...New material, yet to be released. Give it a listen and I'll look forward to your comments. Please put it in my sewing room with my other CD's when you're done listening. The Bands I'll hear today are on the enclosed card.*

Save it also. My foot is better today. The left foot is still swollen I'm taking a prescribed allergy drug. Which the Dr. said would take 2-3 days to really get into my system and begin working. I am a little anemic and he gave me a prescription for iron/or told me to double my women's vitamins-I am working at the River Fest in exchange for the reduced entrance fee $10 instead of $35-work for 1 hr. Today I'll wash my sleeping bags and clothes; rest my foot, *take pictures and organize my food. Maybe go to the Hot springs Spa-take a bike ride, if my foot is good, in the afternoon. The people here in Hot Springs are so friendly. Hope all is well at home. I think of you often and look forward to returning. At this point it's looking like the end of May-barring any health issues. Take Care, Love, MOM*

Saturday May 11, 2002 7:45 A.M.

…Went to a festival last night at the campground. Well, let me back up, *first* I went to dinner at the Paddlers Pub. I had steak, like the doctor suggested. You *know* the whole red meat for iron thing. I hadn't had meat for over a month and while it tasted good, I won't be doing it again any time soon. My stomach is a mess, but I got things to do, so…outta bed and walking I end up at the campground.

Now, I want to be legal tonight so, I ask one of the festival organizers, "Do you have any work?"

He said, "Yes" and so it goes. I am now on the work crew for $10/hr., plus admission.

And it gets better, *'cause*, on my way out, I do a little dumpster diving and find two green wrist bands. Score! What a day! Smiling all the way back to the hotel I think: *now I don't have to pay or sneak in!*

All *this* even before breakfast which, by the way, is my next stop… The Smokey Mountain Diner and ah, that first cup of coffee to complete this perfect morning. I meet up with a bunch of hikers. Don't know any of 'em, but it doesn't take long, 'cause as soon as I say my trail name they echo "Oh, yah, read about you and the Nocturnal Nudists."

"Guess we are legend!" I respond with a smile.

"Do you guys really hike nude?" they ask. "Guess you'll have to hook up with us and do a little night hikin' if you want to really know," I coolly answer, so as not to give away any hint of a clue as to whether we do or don't.

Back at the hotel, I take a nap after washing my clothes and the sleeping bags.

Jester walks in. I wake up. He wants to use the bathroom. We talk for awhile.

"Dude, your armpits are hairy" he says.

And I think: *Gee, maybe I should get a razor and deal with them… or not. Hey, why bother? I'm hiking.* So, no armpit shaving here…

Gourmet comes back. We all have a few beers.

After dinner I am going to the music festival called: *RiverFest.* Gourmet and I sneak in through the woods. Hobex.

Just listening to and watching the drummer made me think of home. At the end of the show I went up to him and we talked. He gave me a CD of their yet –to- be- released music and told me that next week they will be signing horns, drums, guitar, bass, vocals. …A five piece band.

Back in the room, it is1:45 A.M. and I am eating, after watching a great band.

Question of the day on peace activists: Should we storm the church or pray they go away?

> we are magnets
> we are energy
> the thread of life flows through us to another side…
> accepting of all
> positive in all thoughts
> we are laughter
> we are tears
> we are trying…
> to walk away
> from Hot Springs

Sunday, May 12, 2002 A.M.

Oh, well. Early morning realizations coupled with indiscriminate whining looks like this: Too many people in the room. I need to go away, now! Start hiking, again. Is it human nature to be human or natural? I am feeling fat. I am hoarse. I have a cough. I need to draw. And, what about that Mammogram stuff? My foot is not better enough. I need help here. I've been off the trail for too long. I want to leave with whoever is leaving: Today.

Home: what isn't strewn around the room; rests beside me and not where it belongs. Patience… I'll get through this, 'cause it's just *another* "day in the neighborhood!"

Who am I, here, on this trail?

Hot Springs: the virtual trail vortex that sucks hikers in ….any moment I could find myself buying a mailbox and running for public office!

A mother on Mother's Day, off the trail, holed up in Hot Springs, N.C.

You come into the room with a package from home.

"Hey, here's a card for yah," you say, as you hand me the envelope from your bump box. The scripted words: *be gentle with your self* were just what I needed…

There is a pool table at the Laundromat. You play pool and I sleep.

When I get up from my nap I feel dizzy and lower myself against the door jam.

I get upset 'cause I don't know what is wrong with me. And as soon as I can, I go across the yard and tell you.

"Well, you're not dizzy now, are you?"

"No," I answer now feeling a little foolish.

"Well then, let's play some pool!" you exclaim.

Which I try for a few turns before, out of my mouth and in true randomness, I blurt out

"Hey! Let's go to the Salvation Army."

"Yah, maybe we can find some costumes for Trail Days," you say.

And I'm thinkin' *nothing like a little rummagin' to cure these health related blues!*

And we're off…

Well, this Salvation Army store is just a little white clapboard garage behind a ranch house, not your typical downtown establishment.

An elderly man unlocks the side door to a mecca of clothes, clothes in bags, clothes in boxes, clothes on hangers, fancy shirts with ruffles, suits, neckties, southern style poofy dresses, beads, toys… and on and on this is a dream come true!

A rummage goldmine… We are excitedly in and out of various combinations of skirts, tuxedos, hats, shoes… I am in heaven! …like a kid in a candy store! We play and laugh and leave with more stuff than we can possibly fit in our packs.

We will be so stylin' at Trail Days!!

From here we walk up the hill to the local school library and I use the computer to look up airfare info for France!

Sunday, May 12, 2002

So, this book is now upside down.
Hot Springs has left its mark on my psyche.
Me. What to do?
Keep hiking.

> unindexed
> precious metal
> in your wool sock sweat- soaked boot
> ridin' free

Tomorrow I will leave Hot Springs, for sure. Yes. I will actually leave this comfortable trail vortex! What will it be like to walk away from this playground, I sit and scribe the very words that describe its action, when from out of the blue comes the feeling of being freer than ever, and yet, scared to move on.

What am I doing? Where is my mind going? Where is my body going?

All I want is to walk in companionship with nature and its solitude.

I must follow the directive and keep walking.

The A.T. It's just a path.

Is that to be feared?

Tomorrow will tell….

Monday, May 13, 2002.

Art: A modernistic interpretation of the essence of form based on spatial realities of shadow, contour, and color. Color evoked by a feeling triggered by its very essence. Art, utilizing colors and form as it relates to spirituality can generate an emotional response.

How is color reassembled in your mind?

How does the eye transfer images to the part of the brain that interprets and organizes it into a meaningful experience?

Associative action of color….

My world upside down... Much like this book… What happened here is… what happened is of its own doing. Letting loose of self imposed control and feeling for once…

Tomorrow… An 11 mile day lies ahead. I will be on my way, again.

Jennifer Blakely… Hot Springs… …this has turned into a zero week… The Ground Hog Day of North Carolina….

Thursday May 16, 2002.

I call your Mom and then call home.

Now, for another one of my random tangents… It looks like I'm going to France in several weeks. Just a little A.T. side trail! Ya, right. More than a point five, though! I am scared, but I think I have to do it. I will go after Trail Days. Just like that. Can I do it? *Oh*, and did I mention that I've never flown…..

Leaving Hot Springs… I am doing the best I can to return this hotel room to its original state, which is no small feat! And now I find out that, the only walkin' I'll do today is down Main Street. No eleven miler; I am taking a van to Damascus in order to make Trail Days on time.

The white van pulls up alongside the outfitters. Half a dozen hikers hop in. …Seems so weird not to be walkin'.

Along the winding mountain road I begin to feel ill.

You coaxingly say, "Tell the driver…c'mon, tell the driver. Don't keep tellin' me."

"Okay, okay," I say, then in a rather meek voice, I ask the driver

"Can yah stop? Please."

"What's wrong?" he asks. No time for lengthy explanations, and with what is now a huge lump in my throat and a beet red face I just blurt out,

"**Sto..opp… Now**! I'm going to be sick!"

You are quiet.

The van stops.

I get out. I do a couple of loops around a tree lined dirt road.

I take a few deep breaths and then re-enter this now quieted road tripping van.

Close to Damascus now, the driver asks, "Anyone hungry? I gotta gas up and there's a fast food place right over there."

Food is not what I'm thinking of, but I go in anyway.

Free crackers… Hmm, that works for me.

Damascus, Virginia, 1,928' 455.4 miles from Springer, is called "the friendliest town on the Trail" and the home of Trail Days, first held in 1987 as a commemorative event for the 50th anniversary of the A.T. [Appalachian Trail Thru Hikers Companion. p.46. 2004 Edition.]

I go to the clinic, but no one can see me til tomorrow.

The Place

Since we are so early, we choose a spot near the fence, under a tree and proceed to set up the tarp. You blow up balloons and hang stuffed animals and other assorted toys along the fence and from the tarp poles. This Salvation Army score has rendered the ballroom palace a rather unique and curious spectacle. Are we stylin' or what? We even set out a little swimming pool to house a case of beverages!

Garish: overly tenacious; that's our tarp on the rue - de - tents!

As soon as the decorating is complete, I crawl into my sleeping bag and sleep... on into the night. I am still not feeling well. My guess it's the allergy meds, anemia, and overall physical exhaustion.

In the same face up flat on my back position that I fell asleep in eight hours ago, I am edged from my deep sleep by a cacophony of hiker banter and general silliness.

"I know where I am. I know what my name is," I amusingly recite to myself.

"Hey, you're awake," you state, as you gently push aside the draped door, then ask,

"You want some pizza?"

Eating's a good thing. Too tired and comfortable to move I watch the world outside my door and write.

I go back to bed at 10 and sleep 'til dawn.

Friday, May 17, 2002 A.M.

I believe that upon waking at 6 A.M. I'll beat the crowd but, the bathroom line is already knee deep. A pink and azure blue horizon is mirrored in the hostel window.

It is freezing cold. It snowed in the mountains last night. You are still sleeping. I pee outside by a truck.

I walk to the local pool and, while readying myself for a long hot shower, some girl says, "You want some shampoo."

"Sure," I answer, in true refuse - nothing - that - is - free - hiker - fashion, while at the same time thinking: *How bad is my hair anyway?*

…at the clinic for a strep test; result: negative. The doctor gives me new allergy medicine, iron pills and nasal spray. "You should be feeling better in no time," he confidently assures me.

Breakfast at the Side Track Café… My stomach is still a tad cranky. As I wait for breakfast, I make a conscious decision not to talk today: my voice shall be quiet. A silly little challenge, but how else can I *think*, which quickly leads to my next thought:

I miss the solace of the trail. More than a week off of the trail and I feel like I'm falling out of synch with myself. I feel disconnected and restless. I want to walk alone for a couple of days.

What about love and human nature? What have I learned about freedom? What do I know about anything? Nothing, I know nothing, plain and simple. I *just… do not… know… anything…*

An ensuing sadness prevails.

We walk through the campground and check out all the venders. From the Natural Clothing vender you buy a mustard-bronze and goldenrod -colored batik wrap. I buy a bluey, peacock -colored print one.

"How does this work, anyway?" I ask. The woman drapes the wrap over my shoulder and around my waist… looks easy enough, though … was I even paying attention?…'cause I try, but…whatever… I'll figure this out later…

I am hungry. …Alligator meat.

"Want some?" you ask.

"No," I answer.

"Have you ever tried it?" you ask.

"No, and I'm not gonna," I clearly reply, as you coaxingly add, "Ah, c'mon."

"What did I say? Did you not hear me? I said, *no,"* and to further drive the point home I add, "and standin' here is about as close to eatin' alligator meat as I'm ever gonna get!"

You buy a hammock, bring it back to the yard and set it up.

I walk around Damascus with various hiker friends. I bump into people from the trail who I haven't seen for weeks.

I eat, again. It's pretty much nonstop, like breathing! My body craves food, sleep, pizza and more pizza. Ice Cream…

Miss Dot's at midnight. I dance to country juke box music at the Laundromat. I sing Rocky Top with you. How many versions of that, are there anyway?

It's *well* after midnight, now, and you have an idea. "Hey, let's change the sign here."

"Okay, I say, as I help you rearrange the letters at the gas station marquee, from I don't know what, to: Shit Now Showing, and think, upon gazing at our handiwork, *Who really has the license to rearrange things?*

Headin' back into town, we score a ride in the back of a pick up truck. What is it about hikers and pick up trucks? …Going back to the river for more music. Just on a roll.

…Early morning now and finding my way to the tarp. … holdin' my own.

Saturday, May 18, 2002. A. M.

It is late morning when I wake up and head over to the Side Track Café. …home fries finally!

…Very cold and rainy. …Hiker talent show at the gazebo. I pretty much have on all that I own. I sit near someone from Maine. He gives me his coat, which I wrap around my legs.

You have magnetic gloves on your feet!

You sing two songs: One rap and the other a friend's creation. Trail Song. I cry.

Prizes for performers run all the way from back packs to socks.

Now for the big event of the day: The Parade.

Not just any ole parade, *it's a hiker parade!*

"You ready?" you ask.

"No, I'm not ready! I gotta get stuff!" I excitedly say, as I turn and dash off to the local store, where I buy sparkly jewelry, bubbles, party blowers, and a bunch of candy.

I return, divide the candy into bags and say, "We can throw candy to the kids as we walk."

"Why do you want to do that? Those kids are gonna be ready with super soakers for us."

"*What?* Whaddaya mean?" I ask.

"That's their fun. They're gonna try to soak as many hikers as they can!" you tell me.

"Well, I'm still gonna throw candy," I say.

I'm kinda gettin' the picture…but really have no clue!

So, here's how it goes: The town has the beginning of the parade with their floats, bands, town officials, and the hikers, *just being hikers,* bring up the rear. …Quite fitting. Costumed, we walk in the parade and throw out candy to the kids. The kids in turn, throw water balloons at us and spray us with their super soakers, *just like you said…* It's cold.

I take as many photos as I can. I just hold the camera over my head and click away.

Whatever I get is the flavor of the day. You march along in your scored Salvation Army suit, smiling and blowing kisses! Looking *quite* gubernatorial!

After the parade I sleep. This day never warms up. …Late afternoon. I go to the park for the music. …Rock and Roll and Motown classics. …My kinda music. I dance and laugh with you.

Jester, Zeus, Corncob, Robin, Golem

"Hey, can we sing a song?" You ask the guitar player.

"Sure," he answers.

So, at the end of the night, we all go up on stage and sing: "Don't You Want Me Baby." 'I was working as a waitress in a cocktail bar…'

A local church group is having a cook out and the food is FREE! I'm there!

Go back to the river, thousands of tents, a sea of color, bonfires, a star filled night.

Hook up with you and go to get more food. At the pizza place Ghetto Blaster comes in. I give him half of my baked spaghetti.

We dance to the juke box. Nil Lara, Bonnie Raitt, Cars, Eurhythmics.

Get a ride in a pick up truck to Miss Janet's drum circle party about a mile out of town.

There it is again. Me: writing about getting a ride in a pick up! Focus, here. Well, this out of town party was crankin'… hundreds of drum playin', crazy dancing hikers, movin' and chantin' around a bonfire. …very primal… I'm trying to take all this in, but not feeling my groove. I decide to walk the mile back to town. Upon reaching the gate three police cars pull up *and*, not really wantin' to be part of any scene involving cops I just keep on walkin.' I get a ride in a… you guessed it… a pick up!

…Back at the tarp. …Peed in the bushes, as the door to the place was locked. …Sleeping bag comfort. I guess you rolled in around four or five a.m.

Golem told me last night that he really wants to recover his soul, write poetry and go to school. So, it came as little surprise that in the pre - dawn hours he left unannounced. …Just walked outta town. Sometimes, that can be the way it is with hikers. When they're ready to walk, they walk.

Sunday, May 19, 2002

At the church lunch with Zeus and Jester.

Zeus recountin' his grandmothers' big Italian Sunday lunches says, "There's Veal Cutlets, Chicken Cacciatore, Corn, Banana Cream Pie, Strawberry Shortcakes, and always, *always* Ice Cream in the frij.

At least two options for dessert, depends on the crowd. If you say you're coming there's enough for fifteen!"

His cell phone rings.

Gram says, "Am I interrupting dinner, I can call you back in minute."

Zeus says, "Gram! Ya kiddin' me. Hey, you guys with the Raviolis…"

You buy me a raffle ticket for a homemade quilt.

Sunday, May 19, 2002 Damascus, Virginia

Today is the day for me to figure things out.

Going away is not feeling as right as staying. I am finally myself or I think I am closer to who I feel I am. What have I figured out? What calls me home?

in a night filled day
darkness
dissipates in a pinwheel blur

Sunday, May 19, 2002 Afternoon

…Quite cold. <u>Downtown</u>: we jump a little train and ride through town to the park. You wave and blow kisses to what we now have come to call, *your people*!

Off the train, I put my arm around you and we head for the highway.

You sit on the edge on the road, *well*, actually you are sleeping on the grass, and I am hitchhiking.

"Do you have a ride, yet? I'm gonna get up and ….

"No, not yet, and don't you get up. Just lie there. I'll wake you up when we have a ride.

Trust me, I'm not gonna leave you sleepin' by the side of the road…" I quickly reply to what is once again your sleeping body.

Finally a car stops. The couple patiently listens and agrees to give us a ride as I add,

"Can you wait one minute while I wake my friend?" I run and try to shake you awake. You are a good sleeper. You are not waking up.

"C'mon, C'mon, wake up! We gotta ride. C'mon. Just get up!" I expressively say directly into your ear and you're still not even moving. Then, finally, finally you open one eye and sleepily ask, "What? What, is it?"

"I got a ride!! Just get up. Get in the car and don't talk," I instruct, as I grab your forearm and pull you up towards the waiting car.

Abington, Va. 14 miles east of Damascus, Va.

"Are you hungry?" you ask.

"Yes." I answer and think: *when is a hiker not hungry?*

So, we go to a supermarket deli and buy and eat among other things mashed potatoes and gravy.

Now we're off to the two o'clock show of Star Wars in a theater that was made especially for its showing!

Nothing like a satisfied stomach, a good movie, comfy seats and popcorn to put me right to sleep!

After the show we get food again, and meet up with some other hiker friends.

"You goin' back," they ask.

"Yes," I answer. And even though we are all fully capable of walking the fourteen miles there is no debate in regards to the question as to hitchhike or walk!

"So," I say as I step off the curb and begin to cross the highway, "I'm gonna get us a ride."

"What? Where are you going? What are you doin'?" You call out.

"C'mon," is all I reply to your fired questions, as I continue in an unstoppable pace across the busy thoroughfare.

You follow.

My plan unfolds as I ask, the first of several unsuspecting gas pumping individuals the following, "Hey, are you going to Damascus? And, would you mind givin' a few of us a ride?" until finally one answers, "Sure. How many did you say? Six... Hmmn... Let's see. I'll have to rearrange a few things, but I think it'll work"

We pile into his compact car, four in the back; three in the front. It's tight, but we're happy to be ridin.'

"Hey, are you guys' hungry?" He asks.

"Yes! We all answer. Hikers are always hungry!"

So, into Burger King we roll. You and the driver go inside.

While we wait, and in an effort to make more room inside the car, Jester opens the trunk and says, "Hey, check this out," whereupon he pulls a chainsaw from the trunk and holds it above his head and complete with sound effects and in true logger fashion he pretends to be sawing!

Amused and concerned at the same time, I'm thinking, *Isn't this the type of thing that might draw attention from, say, the local law enforcement?*

You are outside now with food and coffees. We pile back into the car and head off.

Damascus.

It is still cold out.

"You wanna play cards?"

"No," you answer.

10:30 lights out….

Monday May 20, 2002

In the A.M., I ask, "What about Hot Springs?"

You take down the tarp and clean up the yard. I shower and pack. I put stuff in the hiker box.

You give away the tarp.

"What!! Why'd yah do that?" I somewhat confusedly ask.

"Don't need it anymore," you matter -of- factly answer and I follow with

"Ah, well… okay… but, won't we need it for…" before you cut me off with a concise sounding, "Nope."

Side Track Café: split a cinnamon roll, bacon and eggs with you.

I go to the outfitters and buy a pair of polypropylene liners and a trail day's t shirt.

I do two marker drawings at The Place. …A linear drawing with no lines.

"Can I have it?" asks a guy waiting to transport folks.

"Sure, I answer. I sign and date it, and for some reason I take a picture of it. I do one more and give it to Jester. My markers are pretty much dried up and it begins to sprinkle.

You play baseball with a cinnamon bagel until someone finds the ball.

Miss Janet arrives. We throw the gear in the van and head to Erwin, Tn.

Along the way we stop by a shelter to get Unc's poles, go out for Chinese food and arrive by nightfall.

"Anyone feel like bowling?" I ask.

In a matter of minutes I am changed, in the van and on my way to a night of *extreme* bowling! …Five lanes ten people. The lanes are fantastic! My scores on three lanes: 150,153,157. We all score in the 100's.

Little did I know that bowling was not the only thing on the evenings' agenda, 'cause from the lanes we go to a Karaoke Bar.

We move the tables, sing 'Don't You Love Me Baby' among other titles, take pictures, and just have too much fun, right up 'til last call.

headin' out the door, the waitress says, "This is the best Monday I've ever worked. And, hey, you guys should check out Wednesday Karaoke in Johnson City."

Miss Janet's at three a.m. You cook a lobster, but I am just too tired to stay awake for what would prove to be a tasty feast!

May 21, 2002

I wake up at 7:13 A.M. and begin filling in this journal, the last few pages of it… smell the bacon and listen to the words coming from the kitchen.

Big Boy leaves for Buffalo, N.Y.

To cover room and board I do a drawing of her house and put up some shelves in the dining area.

"I gotta go to Wal-Mart. You guys wanna come?" Miss Janet asks.

"Sure," we answer and we're off to the one store that I refuse to go in: Wal-Mart.

Upon arrival I ask, "Can you bring my film in?"

"Sure, but what's this, you -not- goin'- into- the –store- thing all about?" you ask on your way out of the car.

"A matter of principle," is how I respond to that question and it stops there.

You get me peanut M&M's and more markers.

I need to draw now and ….

Call home and get on with it.

Wow! I haven't written in this for nearly a week. What can I say about Damascus and Trail Days?

Wednesday, May 22, 2002 Curly Maple Shelter. USFS 230, Indian Grave Gap, Curley Maple Gap Shelter: 3070' Nolochicky Gorge, Nolichicky River: 1700' Erwin, Tn.

…Slack pack. …11-12 miles.

Rolling and subsequently smoking oak leave cigarettes you say, "Surprisingly smooth. Kinda has the taste of a burning oak leaf."

"Yah, *think*," I sarcastically shoot back and add, "Sounds nasty."

"No, really, *it's really* not that bad. It's actually pretty good," you half heartedly say, in an effort to convince me, that this spur of the moment idea to satisfy an addictive urge, is really the way to go.

"Ya, sure, whatever…" I say, not buyin' into what the look on your face is really telling me about what these crushed and rolled oak leaves are supplyin.'

Miss Janet's: spaghetti dinner, wine, candles, people, lots of photos.

…random kitchen sound bites…

Steven King: The Girl who Loved Tom Gordon, a girl who hiked the A.T. Magnolia, Cradle will Rock, Bandit: great music, The Rookie: Dennis Quaid, check this out. Kiwi recommends it!

Postcard Home

5/27/02 saw a bluegrass band at the Nolichucky Rafting Center. After a long day of walking. I am loving the whole experience-it is hard work but, the rewards are well worth it. I've been doing a lot of art work here in Erwin. Landscapes based on my journal entries. I'm using markers and crayons! It's looking like June-July at this point before I'm close enough to rent a car and drive home, but we'll talk. I'm in great shape and want to keep on keeping on. . Will call you in about a week. "MadBowler" Love D.

Postcard Home

5/29/02 Memorial Day Weekend

Hi. Great hearing your voice the other day. I've done a 14 mile slack pack day. Curly Maple Shelter to the Nolichucky River. I did go rafting 3 weeks ago and maybe will try it again. Spivey Mtn. Gap to Nolichucky River and then to Beauty Spot. 2 -11 mile days in 80 degree heat. I am seeing mountain laurel; jack in the pulpits, huge trees! Saw a little red snake and a rabbit in my path. I'm thinking of you and will call soon. Leaving Erwin tomorrow Love. MOM.

Friday May 31, 2002. Slack pack. Spivey Gap, U.S. 19W 3252'Ogelsby Branch, No Business Knob Shelter; Temple Hill Gap: 2850', Nolichucky River: 1700'.

I will run this part of the trail today. This lasts just so long in the 80 degree heat and the run turns into the walk for me. Alone; I stop at a clearing and decide to eat and rest. The break subsequently turns into a nap and when I wake up I do not know which way to go 'cause I don't have any idea from which way I came. No Data Book to help me. I wait awhile, not sure how long 'cause I don't have a watch. I begin to walk, quite unsure of my direction, but *hey* I'm on the trail and I should meet someone, *right*? One would think. But I don't. *Finally*, I see the Nolichucky and all is good. It's a long down, with a little trail magic filled cooler at the roadside. I am tired as I cross the steel bridge *and,* as luck would have it there is a church and services are just ending. The *good people* are making their way to their cars and I approach a couple to ask for a ride.

"No problem," they say, and continue with, "Where are ya going?"

"Into Erwin," I politely answer.

Safely back at Miss Janet's and talkin' with Gourmet the conversation comes around to, "What about that book idea?"

"I'm all about it, let's just do it!" I enthusiastically say before adding "You *know*, a book for other hikers, on *how to hike and have your fun...* ...takin' your time... ...experiencing the community life kinda like we did!"

"Or, how about an art exhibit with your paintings from my photos... an installation piece with sound! ...something you could walk into, a total sensory experience!" he excitedly adds.

Words, sound, color....

"Yes, that's it!" I say, then briefly pause and think to myself..., *this experience really has come full circle and I have reclaimed a sense of purpose* ... before resuming the thread of conversation...

radioman
my waist near your arm
you whisper my name and say
"who is going to move barefoot across the ballet dancers' floor
and shed a tear, dear?"
and did I utter, "…that tomorrow's rain won't fall"
and did you assure me
that "all would be right
tonight…."

Sunday, June 2, 2002

And with this entry I can, with a renewed sense of self assurance, say, that my current walk has reached its natural conclusion. Yet, this journey of mine is really just beginning and truly, when all is said and done I can honestly smile and think:

…..no freedom can match that, of strapping a pack on and just walking…..

And hey, *who knows*, maybe I will write a book and send it to that Springer -Mountain- Preacher from Ohio!

Laundromat

Stover Creek

Blood Mtn.

Bear Bag

Bump Box

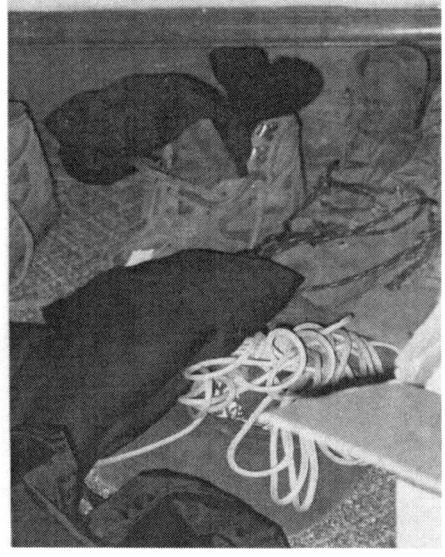

Haven Motel

Socks

Gooch Mtn.

Hogpen Gap

Mt. Cammerer

Albert Mtn.

Bridge Jumpin'

Cold Spring Shelter   Curtis's

Ms. Janet's

Epilogue

Gourmet, Pan, Ashtray, Jester and You periodically meet in Vermont at D's to hike, sit around a fire, eat some good food and basically hang out and laugh.

More specifically:

Gourmet got married. He and his wife completed the Appalachian Trail [Georgia to Maine] and the Long Trail. They spent a summer with D, where she painted several pieces from his photographs, before returning to live and go to school in North Carolina.

You hiked the Appalachian Trail [Georgia to Waynesboro, Va., flip-flopped and hiked from Maine to Gorham, N.H.] in 1999; [Waynesboro, Va. to Mt. Greylock, Mass.] in 2000; and [Georgia to Conn.] in 2002 and work as a fulltime musician in Montana.

Ashtray completed the Appalachian Trail in 2005, moved to North Carolina, completed 1000 miles of the PCT in 2009, and works as a maintenance manager at a resort in Arizona.

Pan completed the Appalachian Trail in 2002, moved to New York City, bought land and built a house in Vermont, hiked Kilimanjaro, and is attending grad school at Columbia.

Jester completed the Appalachian Trail in 2002, moved to Colorado, got married and completed his teaching degree. He and his wife are expecting their first child.

D completed 350 miles of the Appalachian Trail in 2002, is over half way through hiking the 4000 footers in New Hampshire and plans on completing her Appalachian Trail hike in the near future. She, also, returned to college and earned her B.A., has had numerous group and solo art exhibits, is a Special Education Assistant, and is the owner of Gardenscapes: a Landscape / Design Company and Lily Farm Art Cards.

Bibliography

1. Chazin, Daniel D. ed., <u>Appalachian Trail Data Book</u> 24th ed. Appalachian Trail Conference, 2001.

2. Connick, Kyosho, ed. and John F. O'Mahoney, ed., <u>Appalachian Trail Thru-Hikers' Companion</u>. Harpers Ferry: Appalachian Trail Conference, 2004.

3. Coriell, Jack, ed., and Alan Duff, ed., Dick Ketelle, ed., Nancy Shofner, ed. <u>Appalachian Trail Guide to North Carolina-Georgia</u> 11th ed. Harpers Ferry: Appalachian Trail Conference,1998.

4. Edgar, Kevin, ed., <u>Appalachian Trail Guide to Tennessee-North Carolina</u> 11th ed. Harpers Ferry: Appalachian Trail Conference, 1995.

5. Lauper, Cyndi and Robert Hyman. <u>Time after Time</u>.

6. Ruiz, Don Miguel. <u>The Four Agreements.</u> California: Amber-Allen Publishing, 1997. P.8.

CPSIA information can be obtained at www.ICGtesting.com
Printed in the USA
269295BV00004B/1/P

LU0005442 3719